Charles Agyemang Anto

FOREWORD BY APOSTLE EDMUND APPIAH

Right Time, Right Love

SINGLES GUIDE TO ATTRACTING THE RIGHT LOVE

Right Time, Right Love

ISBN: 978-1-916692-36-7

Cover/Layout Design
Equip Publishing House

Published in the United Kingdom by
Equip Publishing House

DEDICATION

To Esther Antwi, my remarkable mother, who raised eight children with love, perseverance and hard work. You always encourage us to be strong and never give up. Your endurance in your own struggles, and several family losses has helped me stand in difficult times. It has also helped shape my growth and maturity. I truly appreciate you, mother!

And to Phyllis — the love of my life, the mother of our three children, and a guiding presence to many others beyond biology. You have been my pillar, my partner, and my unwavering support in this marriage ministry. As an extraordinary mother, you have nurtured and shaped our children with grace and godly wisdom.

CONTENTS

SECTION THREE

SECTION FOUR

SECTION FIVE

ENDORSEMENTS & COMMENDATIONS

In the words of Henry Van Dyke:

"Time is too slow for those who wait, too swift for those who fear, too long for those who grieve, too short for those who rejoice—but for those who love, time is eternity."

Love and time are inseparable. That is why the Song of Solomon warns, "*Promise me, O women of Jerusalem, not to awaken love until the time is right*" (Song of Solomon 8:4).

The timing of the choices we make each day shapes not only our relationship with God but also the quality of our human relationships. In *Right Time, Right Love* you'll discover practical keys to safeguard and strengthen your love life.

Seek God. Prepare well. Stay pure. And relish the blessing.

Singles who apply the wisdom in this book will find a more fulfilling, passionate love life and a deeper, more authentic relationship with God and others. Your marriage need not be average or just another statistic. Step into the marriage you've always desired—starting now. More power to you!

Dr. Nana Adom
Senior Pastor, Grace Community Church,
Redhill, UK

I just want to take a moment to say thank you, and may God richly bless you for writing such an insightful and Spirit-led book. *Right Time, Right Love* truly spoke to my heart. It is not only easy to read but also full of wisdom, encouragement, and truth—so relevant in today's world, especially for young people navigating love and relationships.

We bless God for your life!

The way the author connects with readers is beautiful—it feels as though he understands exactly what you're going through and the questions you might have about love, relationships, and waiting on God.

What I appreciated most is how practical and relatable the book is. It doesn't offer vague theory; instead, it gives clear, biblically grounded insight on how to approach relationships in a healthy, God-honouring way. The message of trusting God's timing stood out and reminded me that rushing ahead of His plan often leads to unnecessary heartache.

I believe every young person should read this book. It provides valuable perspective on choosing the right partner and the dangers of making rushed, unwise decisions—emotionally, spiritually, and even financially. This book encourages reflection, patience, and seeking God first before making one of life's most important decisions.

I highly recommend it to anyone navigating singleness, dating, or simply seeking to understand love from a godly perspective.

Hilda Blankson
London South Area Women's Secretary,
The Church of Pentecost (UK)

Humankind was made to be gregarious. It is part of our very nature to associate with others and form relationships as we journey through life.

When it comes to romantic relationships between men and women, the path can be fulfilling and joyous—or fraught with danger, heartbreak, and scars.

Charles Agyemang Anto's timely book, *Right Time, Right Love,* offers insightful guidance for singles navigating the often complex road to lifelong commitment. He teaches crucial steps—self-discovery, self-acceptance, emotional maturity, and healing from past hurts—essentials for building healthy, godly relationships.

Excellence in any area of life requires preparation and knowledge. This book is a powerful tool from a seasoned author, and a must-read for anyone who takes life and love seriously.

Dr. (Mrs.) Grace Asante-Duah
MBChB, Specialty Registrar in Obstetrics & Gynaecology
Minister's Wife, CoP UK
Published Author
Conference Speaker & Coach

This book is timely as it brings to the fore challenges faced by young adults preparing to date and ultimately to choose their lifelong partners. It gives insight, wealth of advice to would be partners. When growing up, there were things we could not ask our parents due to our cultural orientation, and the fact that you could be punished for even asking. This meant learning as you go, which with its pitfalls, lead to accepting certain practices as normal.

These concerns are expertly laid out in this book with adequate lived experiences, as well as solutions and recommendations. Some of the examples reflect a common thematic area which many of my friends and young adults have asked me about. I believe the solutions are found in this book as it lays bare all the needed information required to help would-be couples embark on their dating journey.

Every chapter is backed by scripture and sows the seed of the word of God in the spirit of the reader. The Author reveals the rules and conducts of Godly dating, the most important and controversial topic of purity and sex, which will allay the fears of would-be Christian lovers. It concludes with a clarion call for would-be couples to invest in love.

Anita Ephraim
Presbyter Crawley PIWC,
Church of Pentecost UK
Social Worker - UK

In a world filled with noise, pressure, and confusion about relationships, *Right Time, Right Love* stands out as a clarion call to return to God's timeless principles for love, dating, and marriage.

Charles Agyemang Anto writes with clarity, grace, and biblical conviction. This book is not just theoretical—it is deeply practical, addressing the real issues singles face today. It challenges readers to build not just romantic relationships, but God-honouring ones founded on purpose, purity, and patience.

I wholeheartedly recommend this book to young adults, church leaders, and anyone guiding others through the journey of singleness and courtship. It is a treasure of truth and counsel that will help many avoid heartache and discover God's perfect timing for love.

Kingsley Akowuah
Pastor, Christian Family Church,
Woking, United Kingdom

Right Time, Right Love – Indeed this book simplifies the art of dating, breaking it down to the dos and don'ts, interspersed with practical guidance on how to find the right partner, and journey through life with your partner.

The text practicalizes how to love one's self, going through learning, and preparing yourself for the marriage Journey. It guides the reader on how to achieve same and what they could take to the marriage. The writer delves into a delicate subject of finance and how couples should approach their finances to avoid the shock of contributing to the maintenance of the home.

The author draws the reader through the Maxims of independence, interdependence, and dependency, and subtly ushering the reader to maturity and how to live with people, and then concludes by drawing the individual to the state where you are ready to make the choice, taking into cognisance, your preferences, and choices.

The Book concludes with characteristics and traits of the right woman and man you should marry, drawing various attributes the writer considers important to help navigate this critical and important stage of dating and marriage. The dexterity of the writer, lays bare these considerations and helps the reader overcome their challenges in choosing the right partner. Most importantly, the red flags are clearly pointed out, although not exhaustive, the writer advances the common and ignored warnings, and encourages the reader to lean on the Holy Spirit to guide them, through dating to making the right choices and saying I do. I highly recommend this book to the youth and the young adults about to take the leap of faith into dating and ultimately, to marriage.

Kobby Ephraim
Presiding elder of Crawley PIWC, Church of Pentecost UK;
Director, Alpha Mortgage Services LTD UK

ACKNOWLEDGEMENTS

To God Almighty, the invincible and the only wise God, the source of all wisdom and mystery be glory and honour.

I am truly grateful to Apostle Edmund Appiah, the Area Head for the London South Area of Church of Pentecost, UK for accepting to write the foreword for this book. Apostle also painstakingly read the full manuscript and offered great insights and correction despite all his busy schedules. Papa, may the Lord reward you and give you pleasant surprises beyond your wildest dream!

I am also grateful to my district pastor, Rev Raphael who also took time to read the manuscript and offered great counsel.

Thank you to my niece, author and scientist, Adjoa Sarfo Bonsu for taking time to read the manuscript and correcting grammatical errors.

Special thank you to the following people who read the manuscripts and provided me with readers comments: Rev Dr Nana Adom, Pastor Kingsley Akowuah, Dr (Mrs) Grace Asante Duah, Elder Kobby Ephraim, Mrs Anita Ephraim and Mrs Hilda Blankson. May the Lord bless you all.

To my amazing family, Phyllis my wife and all my children; Elder Adu Kyeremeh, Esther Adu Kyeremeh, Charles Junior, Maame Yaa, and Nana Afriyie Agyemang for reading through the manuscript, correcting and providing support, God bless you all!

To all of you who sit with me and tell me all your stories – your pain, horror and anger. I feel privileged that you trusted me with your secrets you are unable to share with anyone. I am deeply indebted to you.

FOREWORD

It is with great honour and joy that I write this foreword to *Right Time, Right Love* by Charles Anto—a timely, thoughtful and much-needed contribution to one of the most pressing conversations in our time: love, maturity, and marriage.

We live in a generation that is bombarded by conflicting messages about love, dating, and relationships. In our media-saturated world today, romantic ideals are often shaped more by social media, reality shows, and cultural trends than by divine wisdom and sound counsel. The pressure to fall in love, get married, or simply not be left behind can be overwhelming—especially for Christian singles navigating these waters without a clear road map. In this fog of confusion, this book shines as a beacon of light to those who are prepared to follow the guiding principles the author offers.

Charles Anto brings to this work not only his pastoral insight and biblical understanding, but also his deep compassion for the young and single. He writes not to judge, but to equip; not to condemn, but to clarify. With honesty and warmth, he addresses the often-avoided questions: *Am I ready for love? How do I know it's the right time? Is this person truly for me? Have I matured enough—emotionally, spiritually and relationally—to build a lasting marriage?*

What makes *Right Time, Right Love* particularly valuable is its holistic approach to the subject matter. It does not simply offer formulas or steps, but delves into the heart and soul of the reader. This is not a book about quick fixes. It is a call to deep, personal preparation: to be healed, whole, and wise before stepping into the sacred journey of love and marriage. It invites the reader to examine themselves, their past, their values, and their spiritual foundation.

The real-life stories interwoven throughout are not only relatable, but powerful tools for relationships. Pamela's story in the Introduction among others, gives voice to the struggles many face in their relationships. These are not fictional or imaginary stories and theories, but the lived experiences of real people who loved, lost, waited, or chose wisely. They serve as both warning and inspiration—reminding us that love without wisdom leads to heartache, but love with maturity leads to joy and stability.

This book is also refreshingly practical. The checkpoints, reflections, and thought-provoking questions make it not just a book to read, but a manual to work through. It offers tools not only for singles, but also for parents, mentors, church leaders, and even married couples seeking better understanding of love and responsibility.

Charles is right in saying that "there is no luck in a good marriage." Strong marriages are built with intention, preparation, sacrifice, discernment and willingness to learn, adapt and grow. *Right Time, Right Love* gives readers a clear picture of what this looks like in real life settings. It is rooted in Scripture, steeped in truth, and delivered with pastoral care and urgency.

I believe this book will impact many lives, especially in a time when emotional immaturity, fear of missing out, and misplaced expectations have led many astray. It offers a better path—not the easy one, but the right, enjoyable and peaceful one. As an apostle of God's church, I wholeheartedly recommend this book to every single adult, youth leader, parent, and church worker. You will not only gain wisdom, but be empowered to walk in it.

To the precious reader: May the pages of this book be a mirror, a mentor, and a road map. May it guide you to the right love, at the right time, for the right reasons. And may your future relationships be one blessed and blissful, not by chance, but by preparation, prayer, and divine timing.

Apostle Edmund Appiah
Area Head, Church of Pentecost
London South Area

INTRODUCTION

THERE IS A TIME TO LOVE.

> *"He who has never loved has never truly lived."*
>
> *There is a time for everything, and a season for every activity under the heavens: "A time to love and a time to hate, a time for war and a time for peace."*
>
> ECCLESIASTES 3:8 NIV

Love is not just beautiful; it is what gives us meaning and purpose in life. Life without love is not just boring, but it is a meaningless chore!

But in a world where everyone longs to love and be loved, many young singles in their haste, fall into ungodly relationships—often leading to heartbreak, confusion, and painful consequences.

Listen to the counsel by the author of Songs of Solomon:

> *"Promise me, O women of Jerusalem,*
> *not to awaken love until the time is right."*
>
> SONGS OF SOLOMON 8:4 NLT

This timely counsel raises several questions.

- What is the right time to awaken love?
- Who should be the right person for me to love?
- How do I prepare myself before I love and ultimately marry?
- How do I know the right person to choose?

And many more ....

Choosing to love the right way and the right person is not just right; it is what you deserve as a child of God. But that process and journey is not always a straightforward one. It requires physical, mental and spiritual preparation. Whether you are choosing or someone is choosing to love you, you must first be ready!

Pamela, a third-year medical student, shares her journey:

"Growing up in a strong Christian household with my parents helped me to become a strong Christian. I love prayer and the word of God. We would always have family service led by my father. I have always believed that God would help me to choose a partner when the time was right. But I hated men approaching me every now and then. I have had men following me, asking me for my contact and some asking me directly if I have a boyfriend. It has created in me resentment for men.

But everything changed in my second year at the university. I met Frank.

He was the secretary of our Christian Society. Tall, slender, soft-spoken, with eyes that held quiet warmth. His humour, his smooth-pressed clothes, his easy elegance—everything about him drew me in.

But of course, I ignored the feeling. I buried it. It was lust, right? A sin. Besides, he didn't even know me. He would never choose me. Many girls in the fellowship would choose him.

Many thoughts run through my mind. Should I pray to God for him to choose me? Should I approach him myself? What happens if he says no? I chose to ignore all my feelings and allow God to do His work.

Until that day.

Anna, my closest friend, didn't attend our Christian Society meeting, so I was walking alone back to my hostel when I heard footsteps behind me.'Hi, my name is Frank. And you are?'

'Pamela,' I said, heart racing.

'May I walk you back to your hostel?'

I nodded. My hands were sweaty. My voice stuck in my throat. I said 'yes' to everything he said. Until he asked:

'Are you happy for us to get coffee on Saturday?'

I froze. I hate coffee. But I didn't want to disappoint him.

'I don't drink coffee,' I said nervously. We agreed to go for lunch on Sunday after church instead

From Friday to Sunday felt like eternity. I couldn't sleep. I was nervous. Excited. Terrified. Is this what they call love? I asked myself.

He picked me up in his old Nissan Micra, but he smelled divine. I was dressed in tight fitting black dress. When I entered his car, he exclaimed!

'Wow,' You look stunning. Truly beautiful.'

After the lunch, he turned to me and said,'Oh, that God would let me see you every day. You've captured my heart.'

I lowered my eyes, shy but smiling.'Me too,' I whispered. Frank said, can I tell you something? I have been praying for more than two months, and I am convinced we will make a great couple. I nearly fainted! I was blushing. It didn't seem real. Is this divine orchestration? It felt like a dream! Best moment of my life so far! The man I want to choose has chosen me!"

"My problem with dating- Continues Pamela ...

Since that day, our love has grown deeper. But there's a promise we made—to wait until marriage. This is the problem!

He has one more year to graduate. I have two years!

Every time I see him, I ache with desire. But I must always remember our vow and pray—every single day—for strength not to fall.

This is my first relationship, so I often wonder: is this the kind of relationship that leads to marriage?

Have I chosen rightly? Or am I the right choice for him? To God be the glory, our love blossomed, and we got married a year after my graduation.

We are married for 5 years now and are blessed with two children. Frank has become the best thing that ever happened to me"

Falling in love seems like a new university!

And yet, dating the right person gives life new meaning. Their affection fills your day with light. Their voice becomes your peace. Love feels great when you choose rightly!

This is the reason why this book is so important. To answer your questions on how to prepare yourself to choose rightly and how to date with purity, confidence and peace of mind!

Marriage is still hard work even if you fall in love with the right person. It becomes even harder when you fall in love with the wrong person. But do you know how to prepare yourself to become a good and attractive husband or wife-material?

Do you know how to prepare yourself to spot the best person that is good for you?

Falling in love with the right person gives you a better chance for a happy marriage. But this should never be left to chance. You have a huge role to play. After all, it is your life and destiny.

You have a duty to prepare yourself to become attracted to the right person at the right time! This is because there are consequences to falling in love with the wrong person.

Well-wishers with good intentions for you such as uncles and aunties may put pressure on you to marry regardless of whether you are ready or not. They may even go ahead and match you with other suitors. That is not wrong per se but are you ready?

The truth is, there is no luck in a good marriage! It requires intentionality – in preparation and in willingness to put in the shift!

Marriage of today requires both husband and wife to have equal and shared responsibility in every aspect of the home-including household chores, nursing babies and working to bring money home.

It is therefore vital for parents, guardians, trainers, to train and prepare children in their care to make them attractive and loveable!

Young people must build themselves up, physically, mentally, and spiritually before they awaken love.

This book is a powerful guide on how to prepare yourself, assessing your maturity and how to differentiate between genuine love from fake love. It will help you to train yourself to be a great marriage partner.

Who else can benefit from this book?

Parents. It is a guiding principle for parents and would-be parents. It will help you to train your child to make them attractive and desirable for love.

Church leaders and ministers. It will help you to prepare your messages and teachings to equip them for every good work, physically, spiritually and emotionally for love.

Couples who are already married. It can serve as a lens to understand why your spouse is behaving the way they do. It will give you a new perspective on them. It will help you to be more pragmatic in your expectations.

Topics treated in this book include:

This is Love. You are looking for love, but what type of love are you looking for? When they say they love you, can you tell if their love is genuine?

Loving First Yourself. You are the subject matter of this book. How much do you love yourself? This section will help you to become a 'love magnet'.

Maturity. This section is deep. It will open your eyes to several things you have never thought about before. Am I mature? What do mature people do? You will know the signs of maturity. You will also weigh yourself against the maturity scale.

Spiritual and emotional maturity. Maturity is not only physical. To marry and live at peace with another human being requires emotional and spiritual maturity. How much are you prepared in this area?

How to choose rightly. To be married, you must not only choose, but you must also be chosen. This section is full of nuggets to help you choose the right person. It will also prepare you to be attractive.

- **Qualities of right man to choose**
- **Qualities of right woman to choose**

Then finally, the area most of you have been waiting for, **Dating**!

- **Explores the differences between courtship, arranged marriages, and contemporary dating**
- **Rules for godly dating**
- **Unveils the red flags and "ugly sides" of dating**

I invite you to read with an open heart—willing to learn, reflect, and surrender to God's wisdom.

Take time to pause at the **checkpoint questions**. Be honest—with God and with yourself.

Prepare well. Choose well. Date wisely.

And may God bless you as you begin this journey of the heart.

SECTION ONE

PREPARE FIRST YOURSELF

CHAPTER 1

Love First Yourself

"For we are God's handiwork, created in Christ Jesus to do good works, which God prepared in advance for us to do."

EPHESIANS 2:10 NIV

"Remember, you have been criticizing yourself for years, and it hasn't worked. Try approving of yourself and see what happens."

LOUISE HAY

One of the biggest issues many young adults struggle with continuously is the pressure of being like someone else. Not accepting who you are and believing that you are not good enough! When you are an adolescent or a teen, you are criticising every part of your body, action, and behaviour. You think your friends are better-looking, more intelligent, and more privileged than you. Sometimes you compare your nose, then your thighs or the shape of your head, and worst of all, your skin colour. This is a daily challenge that the youth face. They do not love themselves!

I know some young Black people who get very offended when you call them black. They think they are not black, rather they are brown. Some people do not like their height and size, thinking they are either too thin or too big. Others again think they are either too tall or too short! It is a constant, daily challenge for the youth! Unfortunately, this phenomenon does not pertain only to the youth. Many adults of age also do not like something about themselves.

> *"This is a daily challenge that the youth face. They do not love themselves!"*

I recently listened to a conversation at work between four adult women. All of them said they would never leave a voice note or voicemail for their friends, or anyone else. Do you know their reasons? They hate their voices. They would not want their voices to be played back to them.

It is understandable if young people struggle with their self-image. David, 26, told me this, *"I have been called so many names in my house and every school I attend. I am the ugliest person in the world. It is the reason I struggle to go out. I doubt if any woman would ever marry me."*

When I asked David what people say about him, he said when he was a little boy, he had a little burn on his face which had left some scars. This has bothered him very much. But he says there is not too much he can do about this and rightly so. *"But people stare at me in public all the time, which makes me feel very uncomfortable going out,"* he said.

It becomes worse when a person like David is not appreciated by his own family and friends. Even young people, with no deformities or physical blemishes, are struggling—especially with this era of social media influence.

The impact of social media on the youth is huge. We know that some youths have committed suicide due to bullying and name-calling on social media. Currently, the five biggest platforms are YouTube, TikTok, Snapchat, Facebook and Instagram. Young people live in these platforms 24/7. It is their home. It is their playground! Everybody wants to feel important. That is what both young and adults crave for. For this reason, nobody posts anything ugly about themselves. People post only their best days and best moments.

The so-called social media influencers have also influenced the young ones in both positive and negative ways. Young people want to look the same as their influencers. But what they do not know is that these people also have their own issues which they do not expose in public. If you are planning to get into any relationship, you need to accept who you are first.

It is important to emphasise that you cannot expect someone to love you if you don't love yourself. Accepting your uniqueness and the grace you carry is the first step in loving yourself.

Recently a 29-year-old lady, we shall call her Rosa, called me with a serious issue. This is what she said: "Life is hard for me. My relationship is not working, and I am frustrated. My mother is also putting pressure on me to marry. I want to visit him so that he can sleep with me and get me pregnant. After all, that is what my mother wants."

> ***"Accepting your uniqueness and the grace you carry is the first step in loving yourself."***

I asked her how many relationships she had been involved in before she met this man. She said this was her first relationship, but it has been off and on for the last five years. I asked again if she had considered breaking this relationship and giving herself a fresh start. The answer she gave frightened me, "*No papa. This is because no one will date me. I am not nice*"

When a person accepts that she is not good, she will accept any person who they meet on the street who says I love you. If a person looks down upon themselves, they accept anything thrown at them. This is what I call low self-esteem! It is a lack of confidence. They have no value of themselves. Such people can be bought for nothing. They are unable to say no to anyone. They do not honour themselves. They do not feel they are special people. They hide from people. And they have low motivation to engage anyone. It is sad to say that such people will suffer in their relationship if ever they get into one. They need a total mental and mind shift.

Listen to what the Apostle Paul said.

> *"Do not conform to the pattern of this world but*
> *be transformed by the renewing of your mind.*
> *Then you will be able to test and approve what God's*
> *will is — his good, pleasing and perfect will."*
>
> ROMANS 12:2 NIV

This is also the work of God through the power of the Holy Spirit. Counselling with a Christian counsellor can also help. Every child of God must understand that they have been created with all the physical and spiritual qualities to do good works.

"If a person looks down upon themselves, they accept anything thrown at them. This is called low self-esteem! It is a lack of confidence."

HOW CAN YOU IMPROVE YOUR PHYSICAL APPEARANCE

No marriage takes place without your physical body. You can be the most powerful spiritual man that ever existed, but in marriage, you need your body. Your body must be attractive and in good health for your spouse.

A lot of activities in life require the use of your physical body, rather than spiritual. Great men of God and women of God get married to people who are physically attracted to them.

People are paying huge sums of money to improve their looks. Exercise, body fillers, creams, food and all kinds of methods are being employed to make them look great. Some ladies will not leave their homes without makeup. They want to be as attractive as they can!

Cindy, 31, said, "When I was younger, I got criticised a lot for not being beautiful. Since the age of 13, I have always used makeup from my mother's wardrobe. Men have found me attractive with my makeup. My husband says he finds me attractive with makeup and pretty dresses. I will not be confident without makeup. I am always conscious about my physical appearance. It is one of the reasons we are always late to church."

Similarly, good-looking men are also attractive to women. That is why young men also need to look after themselves well. Men who look good and clean-shaven receive a lot of compliments and attention from the opposite sex. Just as you appreciate young ladies who appear great, so the young ladies also appreciate good-looking young men. You cannot be careless looking, wretched in appearance and expect a decent woman to say "Yes, I do," to you. You will attract the type of ladies who are like you.

"You will attract the type of ladies who are like you."

EVEN GREAT MEN OF GOD PREFER GOOD-LOOKING PEOPLE

The reason why physical appearance is so important is not difficult to explain. Our sights were given not just to see, but to appreciate beauty. It is the number one thing people look for when they want to go out with you. You must be physically attractive to them.

Let's see what Prophet Samuel even did:

> *"But the Lord said to Samuel, 'Do not consider his appearance or his height, for I have rejected him. The Lord does not look at the things people look at. People look at the outward appearance, but the Lord looks at the heart."*
>
> I SAMUEL 16:7 NIV

Samuel, the prophet of God was sent by God to select the next King of Israel. A task that was so huge that it would eventually determine how God's nation would be governed. Don't forget that this is the same Samuel who has known God and heard his voice from childhood. He was not a novice about spirituality and the things of God. He understood the gravity of this assignment. **Yet Prophet Samuel, judged a good king not by the heart, but by stature, physique, height, and probably their complexion.**

"When they arrived, Samuel saw Eliab and thought, "Surely the Lord's anointed stands here before the Lord."

1 SAMUEL 16:6 NIV

Prophet Samuel saw a handsome, tall and good-looking man, Eliab. Had God not intervened, Samuel would have anointed him to be the next king. So regardless of your spiritual maturity, you need to impress someone physically to gain attention. *Whether it is a beautiful face, cute stature, sweet voice, long legs, good lips, good chest, nice beard or other features, you must catch someone's attention.*

Eliab probably had a nice beard, strong upper body and handsome face, just as the boys do nowadays. It made him attractive to many people, including the prophet of God!

***Do not judge a book by its cover, they say.* But I am afraid human beings, men and women regardless of their spiritual maturity, do judge a book by its cover.**

If men of God are attracted by looks, can you imagine what other men and women would do? Will you be surprised if the girls in the town also fall for Eliab? Give it a go and try to improve your looks!

HOW YOU CAN IMPROVE YOUR ATTRACTIVENESS

I am sure you like good and beautiful things and so do the people who want to marry you. If you are lucky to be blessed by great looks, which I am sure you are as a child of God, you must make it count. ***As long as we live on this planet, human beings will always be drawn to people who look great.*** It is therefore important to consider anything that helps you improve your looks and appearance. I do not mean augmenting surgeries, but basic care for your skin and body.

Appearance can be a love magnet! Improving your physical attraction will make you become a love magnet! It will improve your chances of getting dates! Not just anybody, but the women and men of God you so desire. After all, they all judge a book by its cover!

The following activities will help you improve your physical appearance a great deal.

1. Healthy Meals for Better Skin

We live in an era where fast food is so common on the high streets. Fried fast food tastes good. But remember they are usually prepared with low-grade chicken and dirty oils. These dirty oils have so many free radicals which are not good for your health. Sometimes when I stand behind the counter, I watch the restaurant's chef using the same oil to fry several chips and chicken. Reusing the same oil to fry things is acceptable, but remember it is not without cost. It creates free radicals, which in turn attach themselves to your healthy cells and lead to diseases.

It is crucial that you learn to prepare your own meals. Not all oils are good oils. Not all meats are good meat. When someone on the high street is picking raw materials to cook fast for you, not only will they pick raw materials easy to cook, but they will also pick low-cost products. They want to make profit from you.

When you eat healthy, with a balanced diet primarily consisting of whole foods in the form of fruits, vegetables, lean protein, and whole grains, they help to improve your skin and immune system. **Fast foods are not just unhealthy, they are also expensive. If you want to improve your body shape and have good skin, eat more fruit and vegetables regularly.**

2. Exercise Brings Attraction

According to scientists, maintaining an active lifestyle with a goal of at least 150 minutes of physical activity a week, including strength training to increase muscle mass on the gym floor, will make you more attractive. Men and women who have toned skin, strong upper body and defined curves are desirable. This cannot be attained by lying on your bed all day long, eating packets of crisps and watching movies on Netflix.

You cannot lie in bed or sit on your sofa all the time and wish for a good and strong physical body. You cannot also desire a boyfriend or girlfriend who looks after themselves well when you do nothing about yourself. Lack of physical activity will make you look older than your real age. There are too many benefits to working out to ignore. The beauty of a young person is in their strength. You can enhance your beauty with jogging, walking, cycling and going to the gym.

John, 30, has a beautiful story: "When I completed university, I weighed 90 kg, and I am only 5.8 ft. I had been eating so much junk food even after university. I felt depressed and demotivated. I did most of my work from home. I would wake up to work and go to sleep at work, all from the comfort of my bed. I would order pizza, chips, and many unhealthy foods. One day I met my friend Joe at work, and he screamed! 'John, what is going on? You are exploding, mate!' This time I weighed a whopping 110kg. He promised to help me out. He would take 2 buses to pick me up for exercises and gymnastics. After 6 months I lost a whopping 30 kg. I felt better. I felt confident going out. I am now going out with Sara, a beautiful and God-fearing woman. But it was Joe who saved my life. My advice to all young people is to exercise to improve their physical and mental wellbeing."

John has a good degree and is working with a reputable company earning a good income! He now has the added attraction of a good-looking young man. No wonder Sara did not waste time saying, "Yes," when she was approached to go out with him.

I know a few people who met their partners at the gym. It is a place of socialisation and connection. But it also affords you the chance to meet people with similar aspirations of working out to keep their bodies in shape. You can find a gym buddy at work, or in the church to go to the gym together. Exercising is very rewarding. It is difficult to start, but once you start seeing the benefits, you will not want to stop going.

3. Good Sleep Restores Your Lost Energy

The importance of having 7-9 hours of sleep cannot be overstated. So many people, including Christians, have been told that sleeping is bad for them. They would rather pray all night or find something to do. Some people even brag about having 3-4 hours of sleep. Good sleep helps to restore hormones, brain activities and key enzymes. Getting adequate rest, which for most individuals is seven to eight hours of sleep daily makes you look sharper, fresher and more alert in the day. Teenagers and young adolescents thrive better on even more hours of sleep. Again, people with very stressful jobs need more sleep to recover fully. Lack of a good amount of sleep impairs your ability to overcome stress. If you want to look radiant and attractive, prioritise your sleep and sleep at consistent times.

"Lack of a good amount of sleep impairs your ability to overcome stress."

4. Reduce Your Stressors

Stress is one of the key things that affect the way you look. It affects your eating habits; and makes you appear unfriendly or less agreeable. Many prospective suitors will be put off by your constant unfriendliness. If you want to look cheerful, agreeable and approachable, please reduce your stressors now. You can also try managing your stress through prayer, meditation, or other relaxing activities. Most of you are working from home all the time. You have no one or no place to vent out your frustration. Please get out of that room and take a walk during your breaks. After work, meet up with friends, go to church meetings or go to the gym. Drink more water when you are stressed. You need to break away from friends and jobs that stress you all the time. Remember, you want to look attractive most of the time.

James said: "I was working for this company that paid me peanuts but demanded everything of me. I was so stressed out working for them. My mood was bad. My face looked ugly and filled with acne. My mother would speak to me, and I would not want to talk to her. One day she said, 'James I can see the toll your job is having on you. Do you want to consider looking for another job?' That night I could not sleep. I was so happy someone had finally told me all that I needed to hear. The next day I resigned. Within 7 days I had found another job. I have worked with my new company for 3 years, and it is the best thing that happened to me. I do not bring work home. I do not stay long hours at work. I have great sleep. My stress level has gone from 10/10 to 2/10. I now have a good work balance, and I can go to church and attend all social activities."

I agree with James, you must either manage the stressors or remove them completely. James chose to remove it. He was a slave to his job that paid him peanuts and yet he was unhappy. ***If you get married to your job, the chance is that you may be single for a long time.*** If your job is too stressful and makes you so unhappy all the time, it is probably time to look for another job!

5. Laughter is Free, Laugh More Often

Laughter and smiles make you so attractive. To be among great friends and family members who make you laugh is invaluable. This is not only free, but it also helps you to maintain good skin, erasing wrinkles and increasing your happy hormones. Life is never intended to be lonely. You must find people within your church, your friends and family to meet up with from time to time.

Do not let your job hold you captive. Be open and friendly. It will also boost your chances of meeting potential good husbands and wives. While people are attracted to happy people, your constant moodiness will repel people from you. Companies want to hire people who smile. Customers want to be served at the till by people with happy faces.

Of course, you cannot be smiling or laughing at everyone, that is insane. But make your smiles count especially when you are being introduced to people, friends and family. Let your genuine smile shine through. Leave a permanent mark in their memory. If they are single let them leave your presence thinking about your smiles and approachability. You will be surprised who will be calling to have a cup of tea or lunch with you!

When we are anxious and stressed, we are unable to smile. When we manage to smile at all, it comes across as not being genuine. When we are holding grudges against people, we appear frowning and unhappy. At that point, we are unable to transmit happiness. I am afraid, you can only transmit what you have! You must be conscious of your emotions and feelings. Your face will always give you away! If you want to be attractive, check your emotions!

6. You Must Improve Your Wardrobe

What you wear will undoubtedly bring a lot of attention, or the lack of it. I do not only mean your outfit or dress, but from head to toe, whatever defines your appearance. For the gentlemen, this includes your haircuts, groomed beard and moustache. Above all, the clothes you wear.

In much the same way, ladies must take great care of their hair and makeup. Making a little effort to appear attractive will most often get attention. I cannot overemphasise the need to wear clothes that are decent. ***If nobody ever comments on your outfit, the chance is that it has no appeal. Maybe you need to improve your wardrobe.***

What you wear will predict the type of people that will be attracted to you. Christians have always been advised to be modest.

> *"I also want the women to dress modestly,*
> *with decency and propriety, adorning themselves,*
> *not with elaborate hairstyles or gold or pearls*
> *or expensive clothes."*
>
> 1 TIMOTHY 2:9 NIV

If you want a true woman or man of God to marry, dressing appropriately is desirable. Choose your colours and your designs well. Men must also not dress anyhow to the public and social gatherings. You increase your appeal with decent clothing.

7. Get a Career, Get a Job

Good careers and qualifications give you a lot of advantages. They help you to meet a variety and diversity of people. It helps you to appear professional and classy. They help to expose you to a large pool of suitors!

We live in a world of shared responsibility between wife and husband. *People with great qualifications and great jobs are always desirable.* Do not use all your time to trim your beard or do your makeup at the expense of your schoolwork and training. **Make every effort to study, train and get a great job. Everyone is attracted to money.**

Anita, 30, says, "My John was not someone I would say was my typical man to marry. I used to see him in church. I would say hello and that was it. John used to give me a ride home after church. My interest grew when I realised that he was an Oxford graduate, working for a great company and earning good money. I don't want to lie, but the day I saw his bank balances by accident, I opened my mouth wide, and said, 'Wow!' Two months later, I said yes to him!"

If you earn good money, drive a good car into your own house, and dress beautifully, who would not like to be your friend or spouse?

8. Talents

Your talents are also valuable and attractive to others, especially to the opposite sex. Are you great with your hands? Do you play any instruments? Can you teach anything? Are you athletic, or play any sport? People are attracted to anyone with any talent. If you can sing, you are attractive to many people. Do not underestimate the power of your gifts.

CHECKPOINT

List all the physical attributes you possess and admire. Don't be afraid to big yourself up. After all, you must first admire yourself.

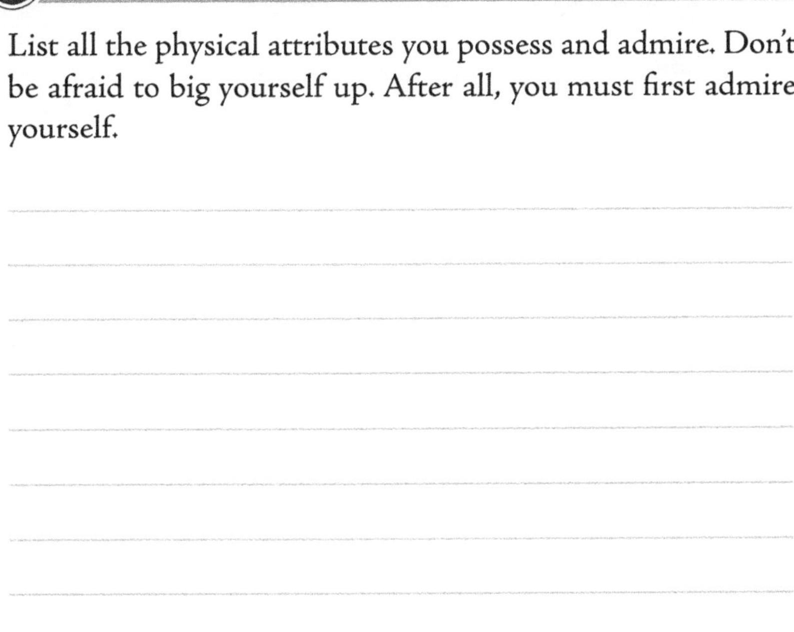

"As long as we live on this planet, human beings will always be drawn to people who look great."

CHAPTER 2

Make Your Soul Prosper

"Beloved, I pray that you may prosper in all things and be in health, just as your soul prospers."

3 JOHN 1:2 NKJV

"For the creation waits in eager expectation for the children of God to be revealed."

ROMANS 8:19 NIV

The essence of this section is to help you understand that you are not just physical but you have abundant talent in your soul and spirit. It is your duty to prepare your soul by feeding and nourishing it with good nutrients.

You were created body, soul and spirit. You are a tripartite being. So, you should not just work on your body, and physical appearance. You must look after your soul and spirit as well. Look into your soul and your spirit to find the great number of abilities you possess. In your soul are the many attributes of knowledge – how you think, how you control your feelings, make decisions – the will, mind and emotions, which define who you are.

It is therefore essential that your soul prospers! If your soul prospers, you will prosper! When any part of your soul is fractured, you will suffer. You will need to work hard to make them all happy.

Maria, 29, married to Demas, spoke of her mental preparation before marriage, "I lived alone after university in a town I knew nobody. I had a lot of time after work. I was buying everything online Amazon, Temu, Boohoo etc. I used all my time and money to decorate my body thinking that would make me happy. But I was feeling miserable the more time I spent on my face, hair, skin and body. Demas changed all that when we met in church, and we started dating. He likes prayer and Bible study. He managed to engage me so much that over three months I had not purchased anything online. When I checked my bank account, I was shocked at how much I had saved! Demas told me that I was beautiful both inside and out, and that I should focus on my inward qualities. Within a short time, Demas and I saved enough money for our wedding. Every young person should understand the benefits of accepting who you are physically and work hard to bring out what is inside you. At the end of the day, your appearance will fade, but it is your inner qualities that will help you survive marital pressures."

The mental and emotional side of marriage is immense and will test all aspects of your mental and emotional capacity to the fullest. When you enter a marriage arena, the pressure is on, and you can feel feisty, and combative. ***Mental and emotional maturity before you marry is not just desirable, it is in fact, an essential requirement.***

Depending on how you get on with the person you marry, periods of mental draining and absolute happiness will vary greatly. *Living with someone and sharing the same space can be fun, but I can tell you that it will also be emotionally draining a lot of times.*

WHAT TO DO IF YOU ARE BROKEN AND WOUNDED

Sadly, many young people have been broken and traumatised by their parents, family members and society that are supposed to protect them. They have not just been failed by these people; they have also been injured emotionally. They walk about with a heavy heart! Their soul is afflicted! *Parents must ensure that children in their care are protected from harm and abuse.*

> ***All children need genuine love, unconditional positive regards or acceptance to be able to grow and achieve their full potential.***

Dana, 42 and married with three children shared her story: "My mother raised four of us as a single parent. My dad was never at home. We have all done well by the grace of God, education and career wise. But my marriages suffered many losses. I am twice divorced. This has affected my confidence and self-esteem. But this started a long time ago. When I was 12 years something happened to me. My mother would ask my uncle who was 18 years old at the time to keep me company until she returned from work. He raped me one day. He told me not to tell anyone if I did not want to die. He kept doing this until I left for boarding school at 15. This traumatised me. I hate sex even in marriage because of the rapes. It is the reason why my two marriages did not survive. I never told anybody, not even my husbands, as I felt so ashamed."

If you are dealing with any form of trauma, especially childhood traumas, they will impact your self-confidence and self-esteem. Prayer and counselling with your pastor or an expert will help you to overcome these challenges. It is important to get this addressed because it can affect your choices and long-term relationships.

If you think badly about yourself, your choices will be bad. If you feel hurt, angry and sad all the time, this will ward off even the people you love. But you cannot let your trauma live with you forever. In your soul are too many gifts and abilities waiting to bless others. You will be a better person, for your spouse and children, if you overcome your bitter emotions and work on your strengths. Focus on all the special grace you carry and let it be the magnet to attract a special person into your life.

> *"Parents must ensure that children in their care are protected from harm and abuse."*

EMOTIONAL AND MENTAL PREPARATION

1. Feed Your Mind And Your Heart With Good Things

Your body receives the signals from the senses and deposits them on the SOUL. Your five senses; ear, nose, eyes, skin, and tongue serve as the gateway to your soul. The soul also deposits whatever it gets from the body to the spirit. Whatever you receive from the conscious mind, from the five senses, will determine your course of action.

If you feed your eyes well by watching films that are spiritual, and edifying, your soul will prosper. What does the Bible say?

> *"The eye is the lamp of the body. If your eyes are healthy, your whole body will be full of light."*
>
> MATTHEW 6:22 NIV

On the contrary, if you're watching dirty films, or reading books that are unhealthy, you are corrupting your soul. If you want to grow spiritually and in faith, you ought to fill your heart and mind with the word of God.

> *"So, then faith cometh by hearing, and hearing by the word of God."*
>
> ROMANS 10:17 NKJV

If you devote your time to listening to anointed preachers, listening to wise counsel or listening to Christian music, your soul will prosper. You are investing well in your future and your life. But if you choose to listen to ungodly music, loose talk, and people who are faithless, I am afraid you are contaminating your soul.

God created our mouth and tongue for many functions. We curse or bless with our mouths. You are judged by people by what you say more than what you don't say. As a child of God, you should train your mouth to inspire and bless. Cursing, gossiping and insulting people are not godly. You can hurt and damage people with your words. You can also murder them with your words.

You can try as much as you can to avoid this, but it may not work if the heart has been contaminated. Listen to what the Bible says,

> *"A good man out of the good treasure of his heart brings forth good; and an evil man out of the evil*

> *treasure of his heart brings forth evil. For out of the abundance of the heart his mouth speaks."*
>
> LUKE 6:45 NKJV

Simply put, you cannot say what you do not have in your heart. Have you prepared and filled your heart with the word of God? If you don't have it, you cannot speak it! When you marry what words are you going to speak to them, especially in times of trials and storms? To be able to speak any inspiration to anyone, especially your spouse and family, you must not just be filled with the word, in fact, you must overflow!

"If you don't have it, you cannot speak it!"

Whatever you are using any part of your five senses to do, remember it is a gateway to your soul and finally into your spirit. Mentally, you must be super sound before you enter marriage. What do you think about all day?

Tom, 39, spoke about his mental health: "Mentally, I am not only weak, I feel I am bruised and battered. I have been through many difficult challenges with my family. I am angry at my mum, my dad and my brother. I am always thinking about how I can pay them back. I want to hurt them. I do not tell my wife, but things affect not just me, it also affects our marriage. I can see I struggle to be open and loving to her."

When your mind and your heart are not in a good place, even if you marry an angel, I'm afraid, your marriage will struggle!

2. Don't Corrupt Your Heart's Drive

Your heart is like a computer hard drive. Your computer will be corrupted if you choose to visit suspicious internet websites. Similarly, if you allow any unwholesome stuff into your heart, you will be corrupted. Listen to what the author of Proverbs says:

> *"Above all else, guard your heart, for everything you do flows from it. Keep your mouth free of perversity; keep corrupt talk far from your lips. Let your eyes look straight ahead; fix your gaze directly before you. Give careful thought to the paths for your feet and be steadfast in all your ways. Do not turn to the right or the left; keep your foot from evil."*
>
> PROVERBS 4:23-27 NIV

It is why you should protect the external outlets of your body.

You are the gatekeeper of your body. *Do not let any unwholesome elements into your soul. They will corrupt your heart drive!* Choose *your friends well. Be careful of what you listen to. Be careful what you watch. Ask yourself, how does this talk, this music or this film edify me?* All you have is your body, soul and spirit.

Your soul will be influenced by what the five senses of your body do. The good and the ugly things that your ear hears, your mouth speaks, and your eyes see are deposited into your soul. This will influence what you think in your mind, your feelings and eventually the decisions you make.

Build a pure and great brand of yourself. Don't ever regret living a good and pure life. There is a great man or woman out there who is looking for your great qualities to marry. God will shine his light on you shortly if you do not compromise!

> ***"Do not let any unwholesome elements into your soul."***

3. Focus on Your Inner Beauty Buried Deep in Your Soul

As a Christian youth, you should understand that God has created you, male or female, with so much more than your physical looks. You are intelligent. You are understanding. You are respectful and you are humble. You are disciplined and self-controlled. You are kind and gentle. You are honest and faithful. You are helpful and compassionate. These inner attributes are so beautiful.

> *"Your beauty should not come from outward adornment, such as elaborate hairstyles and the wearing of gold jewellery or fine clothes. Rather, it should be that of your inner self, the unfading beauty of a gentle and quiet spirit, which is of great worth in God's sight."*
>
> 1 PETER 3:3-4 NIV

These kinds of attributes will take you everywhere in the world. You will be established there as well. ***Physical beauty with defective character will bring you lots of embarrassment.*** Any serious and God-fearing man or woman with a discerning spirit, will hire you above a person who has a good physical appearance but no character. You should focus on building your character with the help of the Holy Spirit until God shines the light on you for a serious-minded person to be enchanted by your inner beauty.

> ***"If you want to grow spiritually and in faith, you ought to fill your heart and mind with the word of God."***

4. Put Your Talent to Good Use. Give Yourself a Chance

You should start to be visible so that the heavens will work to bring destiny helpers your way. *One such helper could be your husband or wife. Idle hands may not achieve anything.* Youths who only hide in their rooms deny themselves great opportunity to meet anyone. Get out and begin to do something outside your daily work. Try sports, gym and social meetings. Try your hands on whatever comes to your mind.

Don't feel shy to be creative and innovative. This is what all people want to see you! Bring that talent out. Even if you fail, it is not the end of the world! Every successful person has failed several times before they finally found their niche.

If you want to be found or find the best person to marry, the best way is to put your talent and gifts to great effect. Listen to what the Bible says:

> *"A man's gift maketh room for him,*
> *and bringeth him before great men."*
>
> PROVERBS 18:16 KJV

Desmond, 26, told me: "My brother Mike is only 24 but he gets all the attention from the girls, and no one looks at me when we are in church. This is annoying. I feel he is sort of taking my shine as the bigger brother."

I asked what he does in church. Des said, *"I am the quiet type, so I do nothing in church."*

"What does Mike do?" I asked.

He says, *"He does everything in church. A drummer, keyboardist, a singer and even ushering."*

I said, *"Ah! That is the secret. You have your own shine, but you are dimming it. He is not taking your shine. Being quiet does not mean a lack of ability. There are so many things you can do. Look for it and fulfil it. And you will see the response for yourself within a short time."*

The whole creation on Earth and in Heaven awaits in anticipation for you to fulfil all the great potential within you. Until you live to fulfil these great deposits of talents, the heavens will not forgive you. Many men and women of God will be attracted to your inner beauty and qualities. Your infectious smiles. Your gentleness. Your faithfulness. Your spiritual gifts of prophecy, visions and working of miracles. Your love and desire for the things of God. These cannot be bought from any supermarkets. It is the reason why you are so unique. You cannot despise these qualities. These are genuine virtues that last long!

> ***"The whole creation on Earth and in Heaven awaits in anticipation for you to fulfil all the great potential within you."***

CHAPTER 3

Passing Your Home University

"It is NOT what you do for your children, but what you have taught them to do for themselves, that will make them successful human beings."

ANN LANDERS

"Do your best to present yourself to God as one approved, a worker who does not need to be ashamed and who correctly handles the word of truth."

2 TIMOTHY 2:15 NIV

Your life is education. It does not start when you go to classroom. It does not end when you finish university. It begins right after birth and will continue until you finally exit this universe. You will be assessed informally at every stage of your life. You will have to pull from what you have been taught, learn and experienced to become approved as a good worker and a good spouse. You will be accredited as suitable and desirable spouse. But you must be tested by your parents, siblings, friends and the person you want to marry. Why should they marry you? What are your credentials? What do you have? What do you know?

Don't leave your parents' house for marriage when you have not passed your home university course! Just like going to university, you do not pass when you have not put in the effort. To excel at your home university also requires effort and intentionality!

When you get married your parents will not go with you. All the things you don't want to do at home, I am afraid you will have to do. Even if you hire someone to do these things, there is only so much they can do.

Areas you need to get a good pass in, include cleaning and organising your room, tidying around your house, using the washing machine, and of course, cooking.

Don't let your mother clean your room for you. Please show keen interest in doing house chores now. Don't wait until your mother or father tells you to hoover. Don't wait for your parents to ask you to tidy up. ***One big difference between a mature, and an immature person, is responsibility or lack of it. Children wait until they are told what to do but a mature person sees things and takes responsibility straight away.***

In marriage, you will have no one except yourself and your partner. They will find you annoying and high maintenance if they must do everything for you. You will ruin the marriage; it doesn't matter how much your spouse loves you.

How is your cooking? Do you buy from the KFC and McDonald's kitchens all the time? Please learn the best and most healthy way of eating. Learn to do the cooking yourself. It will save you and your family money when you marry.

RENT AND UTILITIES

Everything you use at home costs a lot of money. Using water, gas, electricity, Wifi, TV and telephone cost a lot of money. You must offer financial support at home now so that financial obligations will not come as a shock, when you move into your own home. Even if you are lucky and your parents have not asked you to pay anything, please ask how much they pay. You must ask how much it costs to run a home. Make a genuine attempt to pay some utilities.

FOOD BILLS

All the food at home, the vegetables, spices, fruit, bread, milk and different types of cereals are all very expensive, when you put them together. ***Follow your parents to the shop and see how they must balance quality with price to get you good food.*** Sometimes they must bargain in open markets to get cheaper deals. In open markets, you should not pay whatever the seller demands. See how they bulk buy food, and bulk cook as well.

Ask your parents who pays for what, between the husband and wife.

FINANCIALS

Find out from your parents how they keep their income as husband and wife. Do they have a joint account? Do they have joint savings together? What is working well, and what is not working well? What is their advice to you when you marry?

Money causes the most problems in many marriages. If you get a lot of education from your parents, that is a great start. In my pre-marital counselling for couples, almost all young prospective couples have had no hand in financial matters at home. They have not bothered to ask their parents about utility payments, nor rent or mortgage. They also do not have any idea how their parents manage their income.

> *"For the love of money is a root of all kinds of evil. Some people, eager for money, have wandered from the faith and pierced themselves with many griefs."*
>
> 1 TIMOTHY 6:10 NIV

Train your mind on how you should treat money. You also have friends who are married. Open up and ask people about their struggle in handling money. What is your love for money? Do you place your hope and love in money more than your relationship with loved ones?

HOUSEKEEPING

My wife and I travelled outside the country for only 10 days. My daughter was on the phone with us, "*There is no toilet roll. There is no bathing soap. The soap for the washing machine is finished. There is no washing powder. I cannot find any cream for my body. And the food in the fridge is all gone! Mum, how on earth do you keep track of all this? We always have everything here, and now there is nothing here!*" She ended her text with the crying emoji.

If you are not involved or show interest in how your dad washes his car, the chance is that you will not know how to wash a car. If you think the house belongs to your parents and you don't care how it is run, you will struggle to run your own house when suddenly you move out. There are no manuals around that tell you how to run your own home. You catch that by showing interest and being involved.

There are so many people out there who will not go out to buy milk when they use the last drop. Some of you will not buy a new toilet roll when you use the last one. You leave everything to your poor parents to do.

What do you think will happen in your marriage if you leave all such responsibilities to your spouse? Your spouse will find you too needy. They will also be tired and overwhelmed. You will do yourself and your marriage a big favour if you have already learnt to support a home.

HOME RESPONSIBILITY

It is not only about washing and cleaning at home. It is not all about paying rent or mortgage. Just as running a country, so is running a family. There are several departments you will need to consider and support including:

- Order
- Conflict management
- Emotional support for members at home
- Welfare
- Hospitality
- Communication
- Maintenance at home
- Transport
- Recreation
- Entertainment
- Health
- Sanitation etc.

We will elaborate on some of them.

ROLE OF MEN AND WOMEN AT HOME

Order in the Home

Is your parents' home Christian or not? In Christian homes, we expect order and observance of hierarchy. We expect that the father loves his wife as Christ did. We expect the wife to respect and submit to her husband. We expect children to obey their parents as the Bible recommends. Is this order clear and visible in your home? How has this affected you? Have you respected and obeyed your parents? Is this how you want your children God will bless you with, to do? If you do not have this order in your home, how do you want your home to be governed when you marry?

Parents create this order through the teaching of the word and prayer. If you do not have family devotion at home, have you prepared yourself for this when you get married?

Jude, 34, says, "I do not joke with devotion with my wife. We have it every Saturday when we are both home. It has been our unifier. It gets us connected. This I learned to do myself even before I married. My dad always insisted we have devotion at home. So, I have grown with it. If you are not already having a personal devotion it might be hard when you marry. All young people should set time to do this before they marry."

Emotional Support

Life does not always follow a linear curve. During time of losses in the family, such as jobs, confidence and self-esteem, and loss of family members, you are expected to support, empathise and sympathise with them.

If you do not know how to do it, you will struggle in your marriage. Show genuine interest and concern. Be present with them. Everyone can offer comfort in their own small way. When you get married, you will constantly be required to support your spouse, friends and family. Don't shy away from funerals and losses. Your support shows your maturity.

Welfare

Giving to family members comes easier for some people because they come from a large family. They are used to buying presents on special occasions such as birthdays, Christmas, graduation, etc. How involved are you in giving? Are you Mr or Mrs Receiver who gives nothing? Do you get involved in planning for a family member's special day? Maybe you are one of those people who just don't care. If you don't care, you either learn to care now or probably shouldn't worry about dating. You cannot marry if you don't care!

Hospitality

We are all hardwired to be connected to family and friends. You cannot live on an island. You will visit your spouse's family and friends. This is how human beings have always lived. Other people, friends and family members will also visit you. How good are you at receiving visitors in your home? Have you observed how your parents receive and serve visitors? How involved are you in welcoming people into your home?

If you find it a difficult chore to do, this is the time to learn. People will judge you on how nicely, or not so nicely, you welcome them.

There will be days and moments when you are feeling bad, and you will not be at your best, but most of the time, it is expected that you will offer a welcome with smiles. It is critical you appear to be very welcoming and hospitable if the visitors are your in-laws. You do not want them to label you rude and ill-mannered! You should endeavour to be a unifier of your family and your spouse's family. Have you seen how your parents relate to each other's family?

Conflict Management

Things in your marriage will not always go the way you plan it. This can lead to disagreement and conflict in marriage and the family. Do you know how your parents handle conflict at home? Have you taken pains to ask how they have always done this? If your parent is not married, you can still ask your single parent how they did it.

Learning to solve problems in your family gives you a head start in the marriage. Many of you would not have this skill because they aren't taught in school. You usually acquire this through observation and asking the right questions. Be interested in how you solve problems from now on. Problems between your friends and yourself, schoolmates and family members. Show interest in the way individual family members solve problems in the family.

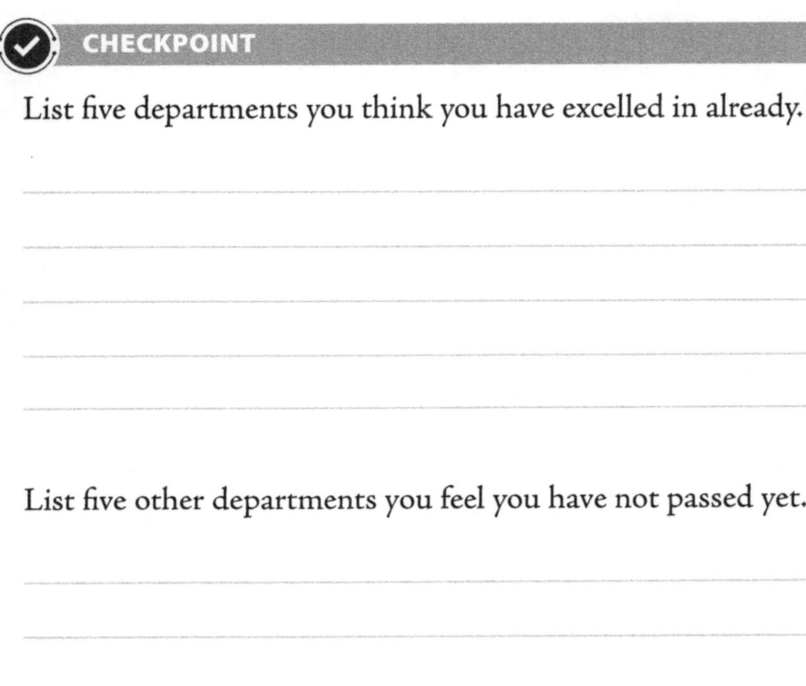

CHECKPOINT

List five departments you think you have excelled in already.

List five other departments you feel you have not passed yet.

> *"One big difference between a mature, and an immature person, is responsibility, or lack of it."*

CHAPTER 4

Build Yourself a Spiritual Fortress

"Marriage is part of spiritual warfare.
Once you are married, Satan fears your alliance.
Whether you know or not, prepare or not, I'm
afraid, you enter a war zone with Satan!"

JOHN HAGEE

"You cannot be a part-time Christian and
win a spiritual battle over full-time Satan."

TONY EVANS

Marriage is the most dangerous warfare you have ever faced. If you are not fully and spiritually prepared, you are in for a rough ride. Weddings are nice and beautiful, right? But that is not "the marriage". ***The marriage is the coming together of the couple after the wedding. If both of you are godly, your marriage will be godly. If both of you are trash, your marriage cannot be any different.*** If you are both prayerless, do not expect a prayerful marriage.

Apostle John admonishes all of us, from children to fathers. But note what he said of young men.

> *"I write to you, dear children, because you know the father. I write to you, fathers, because you know him who is from the beginning.* ***I write to you, young men, because you are strong, and the word of God lives in you,and you have overcome the evil one"*** *(Emphasis mine).*
>
> 1 JOHN 2:14 NIV

I hope this scripture gives you hope. It encourages that once you have the word of God in you, you don't need to be afraid. You have already overcome the evil one by virtue of the word of God in you. **Are you filled with the word of God?**

Many young people have no idea about the reality of spiritual battles. They are so eager to get married. They just love the fun and the funfair of marriage ceremonies. **Some of you do not have quiet time, nor spiritual routines. You just wake up and eat and you are off on your bike.** All that you are interested in is your boyfriend or girlfriend. It is also about the 'likes' of your social media postings! Many are more concerned about social media followings than people who follow Christ. This will not make you strong in the Lord.

No wonder many of you get overwhelmed right after the wedding when the prince of this world, the master tactician, the accuser of the brethren shows up. **He comes to make demands. He comes to test and see if you are strong in the Lord, or one of those leaves that can easily be blown away from just a huff from the nose.**

The following are some of the reasons why ignorant and careless couples fail spiritual tests miserably:

- They are insensitive to the presence of the devil
- They have no ammunition to combat him
- They blame each other
- They do not pray together
- They do not defend each other
- They walk away from each other
- They allow the devil to take control of their marriage

This is because you cannot give what you don't have. If you are spiritually weak, you will be found out. You see, the Bible says,

> *"If you fail in the day of adversity*
> *your strength is very small."*
>
> PROVERBS 24:10 NKJ

Dan, a pastor in Pentecostal church for 10 years has this account, "My first marriage did not work because I was young and careless. I had no prayer, no consultation or proper consideration. Nancy was beautiful and attractive. That was all mattered to me. We had no regard for abstinence from premarital sex. We married and we hit the brick wall in the first year of our marriage. I did not only discover who Nancy really was, but I also discovered my own self. I was a wretch. I soon realised that Nancy deserved someone better than me. We quit after just two years of not trying hard. As a Christian, I live in constant fear and disappointment for disappointing God and fellow believers. Even after sorting myself out, I still feel a failure. I feel I have disappointed Nancy as well. But I thank God that He gave me another chance. He has been merciful and gracious to me."

THREE REASONS THE DEVIL ATTACKS MARRIAGE

There are three main reasons why the devil will not leave you alone when you are married.

1. God said it is not good for the man to be alone.

> *"The Lord God said, "It is not good for the man to be alone. I will make a helper suitable for him."*
>
> GENESIS 2:18 NIV

The devil hates to admit God is right. He is not waging this war against you. He does not only challenge God, but he also wants to prove that what God said is not true. This is the reason why he takes delight when marriage breaks down. He is happy that the divorce rate is high. He is happy that you are not enjoying your marriage. He cries if your marriage is good. He will put in a lot of work to make your marriage look bad!

2. He who finds a wife finds a good thing and obtains favour with God.

> *"He who finds a wife finds a good thing, and obtains favour from the Lord."*
>
> PROVERBS 18:22 NKJV

He wants to prove that finding a wife is nothing good. It is full of tears and sorrows. He wants to ward you off so that God's word will be maligned. Favour? The devil is out of favour! Why would he sit down for you to receive favour? He will battle you and your spouse to steal this away from you. If you are not spiritually prepared, you will give up on each other within a short time of marriage.

3. Being denied of the power of alliance and unity.

> *"Two are better than one, because they have a good reward for their labor."*
>
> ECCLESIASTES 4:9 KJV

The devil knows that when you both are joined together in prayer, he is in trouble. Not only that, but you will also bring forth godly offspring. He hates this, because eventually your offspring will also come and attack him.

So then, you can see that this fight is not against you per se, it is a war against God. It is a rebellion against God. You are only caught in the middle. But all you need to do is to be on God's side. You must position yourself and your family on God's side and He will fight for you.

Don't wait until you marry before you become spiritual. Please begin to strengthen yourself in the Lord.

SPIRITUALITY IS NOT JUST GOING TO CHURCH

Maybe you go to church all the time. You are part of the ushering team. You play instruments. You sing in the choir. You are a PENSA executive member. They are all nice and fancy. It is also nice to be involved. ***You see, the devil is not scared of Christians who just do that. He is not scared of a person who calls himself a Man of God (MOG) or a Woman of God (WOG), yet they are full of lies, deceit, and gossip. If you sleep around with the boys and the girls and still call yourself a MOG or WOG, I am sorry, but you are in the devil's pocket. Your tongues do not go anywhere.*** When you are sleeping around, your tongues are hollow and without power. The devil does not fear you.

The devil fears a Christian who is faithful and practises the following:

- Constant devotion and quiet time in their closet
- Resisting the temptation to sin when no one is watching
- Fasting and praying on their own
- Hungering and thirsting after righteousness
- Faithfulness in small matters
- Not keeping records of wrong against their friends and families
- Being genuine and sincere – their yes is yes, and no is no
- Respecting their parents
- Being kind to their friends
- Rejoicing with goodness and hating evil

This seems a long list, but it can even be longer. If you want to enjoy your marriage, fortify yourself in the Lord before you marry.

CHRISTIANITY IS ACTION

Christianity is a way of life. It is love in action. It is not mouth and tongue. It is what you do with what you read from the Bible. It is what you do with the powerful sermon you hear from the pulpit. It is what you do with the prompting of the Holy Spirit. If people just hear the word and do nothing with it, they become hypocrites. The devil does not spend much energy on such people. He knows they are cheap, light and easy to overcome.

It is your duty to make the devil sweat. It is your duty to make him regret picking a fight with you. Prepare yourself to be spiritually strong to defend yourself, your spouse, your family, and your marriage.

If you are not strong by the time you are marrying, it will be difficult to protect your spouse and yourself.

Peter, 30 and married to Jayne, narrated his encounter: "I followed my parents to church every Sunday. My parents prayed with us children. I pretended to be serious with church but honestly, I did it for my parents. But things changed in my life when I had an encounter with God at university. I was only 19 but the change was dramatic. I was since baptised by the Holy Spirit. I would not have breakfast unless I had my quiet time. By age 21 I was already a PENSA president. By the time I wanted to marry Jayne, I knew Christ for myself. I was spiritually very strong. Prayer, honesty and friendship have been the keys to our happy marriage."

START YOUR DAY WITH PERSONAL DEVOTION

Prioritizing your personal devotion is the greatest way to your spiritual fulfilment. If a Christian youth sets themselves up for daily devotion to connect with God, it is a mark of maturity. It means they take God seriously and I am sure God also will take such people seriously as well.

You do not have all the pressures of parenting and financial responsibilities. You should therefore take advantage of this and grow yourself in the Lord!

KNOW YOUR SPIRITUAL GIFTS

God has blessed all Christians with spiritual gifts. You should be proud of all the great spiritual qualities you possess.

> *"Blessed be the God and Father of our Lord Jesus Christ, who hath blessed us with all spiritual blessings in heavenly places in Christ."*
>
> EPHESIANS 1:3 NIV

Your spiritual gifts do not only give you power over Satan, but they also give you access to princesses and princes. It offers you a lot of opportunities and chances to meet your spouse. You must identify the grace God has given you. Let it work for you. If you still don't know your gifts, you still have time to identify your gifts and use them.

The schemes of the devil to attack young couples are intense and innumerable. So, the watchword is "vigilance". Do not give room to the devil. Be a Christian with dignity and integrity. Do not fear the devil's attack. God will always defend the righteous. Your hopes and expectations will be fulfilled!

CHECKPOINT

What spiritual qualities do you possess that will be great assets to your spouse if you married them? Think also about the fruit of the spirit and the Gifts of the Holy Spirit.

"If you are both prayerless, do not expect a prayerful marriage."

SECTION TWO

MATURITY BEFORE MARRIAGE

CHAPTER 5

Signs of Maturity

"Love is like a friendship caught on fire.
In the beginning a flame, very pretty, often
hot and fierce, but still only light and flickering.
As love grows older, our hearts mature
and our love becomes as coals,
deep-burning and unquenchable."

BRUCE LEE

Every grown-up has the right to marry anyone, and anytime they want. There is, however, a great danger to marriage when couples involved are adults by age but lack emotional maturity.

To be fully mature involves your whole being – physical, intellectual, emotional and spiritual maturity. **Your maturity is not solely in your hands. Your parents, family, church, teachers and close friends all have a role in helping you grow and mature in the right way.**

This section is self-examination and exploration of your maturity before you consider marriage.

BABIES DO NOT MARRY

Babies and toddlers should have no part in marriage. They must wait until they grow and mature. You would not want to marry a baby yourself. You will hurt them. You will also be hurt as well. In fact, the law protects children. God gave Eve, who was already mature to Adam, who was a man, and he took her as his wife. Let's see how the Bible puts it:

> *"That is why a* **man** *leaves his father and mother and is united to his* **wife,** *and they become one flesh." (Emphasis mine)*
>
> GENESIS 2:24 NIV

Marriage is created for a man and a woman. It is for mature people. You need to wait until you are of age to fulfil state laws and ensure you are mature to make your own decisions. You must be physically and chronologically of age. One question that I get asked all the time, is what age should I start dating? What age should I marry?

Legally, in many countries and cultures, you must be 18 years and above. It is a physical and legal age. This is very important. Government and state recognise the need to be physically able and mature before you marry. This is because marriage is for adults. Marriage is hard. But age alone is not enough. You must be mature as well.

Marriage is a crucible, it is pressure. It is a warfare. It can be dangerous. **It can be a death trap. It is an institution which when not handled with care, can break you. It requires a careful choice, daily work, steadfastness and unfailing love to sustain it.** Any mistakes in the selection stage can have a serious impact on the relationship. This is the reason why it requires maturity, determination and prayer at every stage to make it work.

Anna, 26,married to Dan for the last 3 years says, "My first marriage failed not because my husband was bad, I had too many problems myself. I was only 21. I dated for only 3 months and got married. I saw marriage as an escape from parental control. I was not truly prepared. I expected my husband to do everything for me. There was no single day we never argued. In the end, Dan found me too immature and needy. So, after just 2 years we had to separate and go on our own ways. This brought a heavy dent on my character and my relationship with God. I will recommend all singles not to think that sex is enough to make the marriage work. That is immature thinking. Take your time to grow and be mature before you think about starting a relationship."

> ***"Marriage is created for a man and a woman. It is for mature people."***

WHAT IS MATURITY?

> *"When I was a child, I talked like a child, I thought like a child, I reasoned like a child. When I became a man, I put the ways of childhood behind me."*
>
> 1 CORINTHIANS 13:11

Cambridge Dictionary defines maturity as, "***The quality of behaving mentally and emotionally like an adult.***"

This is a beautiful definition. But note, mental and emotional! If you are a Christian, it is also a spiritual quality! But that is not all! **Maturity is not just a quality; it is a PLACE of**

responsibility. Maturity is a lonely place where you will have to make all the decisions your parents once made for you. It is a place where you must cook all the food your parents and siblings once cooked for you.

It is a place where you must wash and clean without competing with your siblings. It is a place where you no longer have the option to either pay the rent, TV license, water, light, fuel, council tax or not. Once you start taking on those responsibilities, we say you are a mature person!

When you choose to move away from your parents' home to bond with another person you barely know, you are saying you are mature enough to manage your own affairs. That is awesome!

Marriage offers you a place where you will have the chance to exercise your gifts and skills of love. But it is also a place where you will have to do all that your parents did for you. You now must behave like an adult!

> ***"Maturity is not just a quality;***
> ***it is a PLACE of responsibility."***

FIVE SIGNS OF MATURITY

People are different but mature people have many things in common. This includes the following:

1. Give and share
2. Desire to serve
3. Forgiving
4. Taking responsibility
5. Emotional stability

1. If You are Mature, Share!

Giving is not just good and godly. Giving is divine. It starts with God who shows us how to love. See what God did…

> *"For God so loved the world that he gave his one and only Son, that whoever believes in him shall not perish but have eternal life."*
>
> JOHN 3:16

Mature and loving people have a free spirit to give. They have a desire to share regardless of how much they have.

Offer a child a toy today. Leave him for a day. Come back and ask him to share the toy with you. You have a higher chance of winning the Euro million lottery even if you do not stake, than the child sharing their toy with you. Children do not share. It is that simple! They do not care that you gave it to them!

Do you know what they do well? *Give me, give me and give me!* They will beg you, and even cry if you do not give it to them. But they will protect what is theirs. This is because human beings are selfish by nature. That is how we were created. It takes training, maturity and the grace of God to overcome selfishness.

But one of the keys to blessing is giving. Givers never lack! If you always lack, check if you are a giver!

> *"I have shown you in every way, by labouring like this, that you must support the weak. And remember the words of the Lord Jesus, that He said, "It is more blessed to give than to receive."*
>
> ACTS 20:35 NKJV

Please do not start dating if you are still protective of your money, food, and your space. All that married couples do is give to each other and share everything, including their beds and their bodies.

> *"But one of the keys to blessing is giving."*

2. If You are Mature, Serve!

Please don't go into marriage with a princess mentality. If you are a prince, please stay in your father's palace. **Marriage is a union of two people who desire to serve each other with love, humility and commitment!**

If you think you will go into marriage to stop washing, cooking, cleaning or working so that someone else will serve you breakfast, lunch and dinner, please think again!

To have the opportunity to serve, places you in the same purpose as Jesus on earth. What did Jesus come to do?

> *"Just as the Son of Man did not come*
> *to be served, but to serve, and to give*
> *His life a ransom for many."*
>
> MATTHEW 20:28 NKJV

You cannot refuse to serve someone you truly love. Serving others does not make you lower than them. **Jesus proved that he who wants to be great must serve. If you are great, you serve!**

I have observed this trend in church. Anytime someone serves in the church it does not take long before they get noticed. They attract even the big men and the women in the church. There is sincere affection for people who do that. They are the ones everyone talks about, especially when it is time to marry.

Freda and Fred came to me for premarital counselling. I remember during one of our sessions, I asked each of them about their expectations in their relationship when they get married. Freda listed about 20 things that she expects Fred to do for her. In fact, everything was legitimate and what many ladies wanted anyway. When it came to Fred's turn, we all expected another long list of what he expected from Freda.

He sat for a moment, cleared his throat and said, "Counsellor, I have come into this relationship with just one motive. I am here to serve. I am here to serve my wife, and the children God will graciously bless us with. I feel I have an enormous capacity to be a blessing to my wife. All I want is that she would provide the room for me to be able to serve her."

Serving offers you the opportunity to demonstrate what you are made of, your character, humility and gifts. Serving is not only a sign of physical maturity. It is also a sign of spiritual maturity.

> *"And since I, your Lord and Teacher, have washed your feet, you ought to wash each other's feet."*
>
> JOHN 13:14 NLT

Maturity is washing people's feet. Washing feet, places you in the same boat as Jesus. It is your passport to greatness! Welcome people with a smile. Serve them with a smile. Let them leave your space with a smile imprinted in their minds all day.

In the church, you have great opportunity to serve. Sweep the church. Help arrange chairs. Help to pack up after church. If you have other talents such as singing or playing instruments, use them in the church. Mature people do not have a frown on their faces when serving or disappearing to avoid serving. They just grab the opportunity to serve people.

"Serving offers you the opportunity to demonstrate what you are made of, your character, humility and gifts."

3. If You are Mature, Forgive!

The ability to forgive others is divine. It is a mark of spiritual maturity. *Every human being you marry will offend you. The relationship will thrive only when you both have the in-built capacity to let go and forgive each other.*

One of the tests for our maturity is forgiving those who wrong you. All praying Christians should not harbour any resentment in their heart. If you want God to forgive you, you must also forgive others. You must forgive your spouse, family and friends. I am sure they tolerate you all the time. They also forgive your weaknesses and flaws.

"... and forgive us our sins, as we have forgiven those who sin against us."

MATTHEW 6:12 NLT

Holding resentment in your heart all the time will destroy your soul. Bitterness is a deadly poison. You have great opportunity to work on your anger and resentment now before you marry. Mature people understand that to err is human, and they offend people and get forgiven. You must pray to God to forgive you, as you also forgive others.

"One of the tests for our maturity is forgiving those who wrong you."

4. If You are Mature, Take Responsibility!

Marriage will make someone your responsibility, duty or obligation to look after. You will take charge of a home. You will look after a baby, a toddler and a child. You must be prepared. You must be ready before you enter marriage. You can decide not to be ready, but it will still be your responsibility. When your child calls, you must respond to them. When your spouse needs help, you must respond to them. You have the chance to grow and mature, by taking responsibility in your parents' home, your school and your workplace.

Areas you can show interest and take responsibility include; paying rent and utility, bills, caring for parents and siblings, washing, cleaning, cooking, ironing and getting involved in family devotions and conversations.

Be keen and active in what parents do. In fact, it is better to support in these areas so that you will not have the shock of your life when you move out. Steve told me his story:

"I got a job in the city after university, so I had to move out and rent my own apartment. I was super excited that finally, I was going to be a man of my own. My mother would not have to monitor my movements. Always checking on me when I go out at night. This really frustrated me. Worst of all, my mother wanted me to hoover the house every Saturday. This I hated doing and I couldn't wait to get my own job, earn my own money, eat what I wanted and sleep how much I wanted.

When I moved out and received my first paycheck, I was horrified. Taxes, rent and insurance meant I was left with just enough money for my upkeep. I called my dad straight away to complain that

I had been robbed. I was angry and screaming. My dad calmed me down and asked me to take a photo of the paycheck and WhatsApp it to him. I did exactly that. I called my dad again in 30 mins time hoping for him to confirm my suspicions. He laughed and said, 'Son, everything is correct. In fact, you earn more than me. You have a responsibility towards not only to yourself but also to the state.' I screamed, 'Dad, this is not fair. I worked hard. I deserve all the money I earn. Why didn't anyone tell me all this?' My dad quietly said, 'Son, you were not interested. Don't worry, you will grow out of this shock. You will be okay. Just reduce your entertainment, going out and takeaways and live like an adult.' I said, 'Thank you, Dad,' in anger and frustration and I hung up.

All the time I had lived in my parents' home, I never paid them much. When I was working in between Uni, when they demanded a token to help support the home, I ignored them. I knew my parents did not earn much, but they coped. My dad is a cleaner and my mom is a nurse. Between them, it was a struggle, especially with three children, but I couldn't care less. Sadly, now here I am, feeling sad and ignorant."

Take Responsibility Now! Please, if you could live in your parents' home, don't abuse the opportunity you have. Make your parents and family feel your presence and absence.

Don't believe me? Listen to Jim, 26, who married five months ago, "*If someone had alerted me that my childhood and youthful life were all preparing me for my career, profession and marriage, I would have taken every instruction and training very seriously. You see, most of us were made to believe that whatever we are doing, we do for our "wicked" parents. We do it begrudgingly.*

I ran away from many chores. I thought my parents were so wicked to make me work at home. I did not volunteer to learn or do things on my own. Even cooking a meal for myself was a difficult task I thought I should not be doing. What about going to school? That was another task that I thought my parents should not force me to do. All my childhood I thought I was going to school for my parents. But of course, I was young, I was immature, and I was irresponsible!"

If you do not help at home, you will not hone your skills or talents. You may grow up with deficiencies in using your hands. You will be so handicapped; you must pay people to help you with basic 'do-it-yourself' (DIY) tasks. It is expensive in revenue. You will save a lot of money if you try your hands on doing many things whilst young.

My wife and my daughter are both hands-on. My daughter, who is a graduate, is such a beautiful hair maker. She does her own hair. I jokingly tell her she is a witch. If you know how difficult it is to plait black ladies' hair, you would appreciate this. Yet she does it all by herself. She is also able to do that for friends and charge them something small. So, you see, she is not only earning money but also not paying anyone to do her own hair.

My great friend Richard is another example. He is so motivated, using his hands since childhood. He not only saves himself money and time, but he also gets money from many friends, by working on their cars for them, including myself. Richard has saved me a lot of money since we became friends. He helps me change everything in my car. He is not only good with cars, but he will also investigate and try to fix boilers, water leaks and many more. He will never send his car for washing. He would wash his car and that of his wife. By so doing, Richard has saved himself and his wife a massive amount of money.

When you always depend on people, it is a matter of time before they start resenting you, unless you start paying them money for their services.

Please take responsibility whilst you are still living in your family home. Don't wait until you are asked. **Start cleaning up after yourself. When you go out, come back with something for the family. Look after your siblings and parents. Show love, kindness and affection towards them.**

Be interested in whatever each member of the family does. Offer them your love, support and guidance if you can. Communicate with them. Don't hide away from them. ***Remember, responsible people share time with each other. They communicate with each other.***

This is your school. Everyone is observing. They will grade you soon. What marks will each of your parents and siblings award you? Let your parents and siblings bear witness when the time comes for you to leave home, that whoever marries you has gotten a great deal. Let them miss you when you are leaving to cleave. ***Let their heart be at peace knowing that you are such a responsible person.***

"When you always depend on people, it is a matter of time before they start resenting you, unless you start paying them money for their services."

5. If You are Mature, Be Emotionally Stable!

To **marry means marrying emotions**. Get ready to manage your own and embrace the other person's as well, if you want to marry. That is maturity. **If you don't want emotions, maybe it is not the right time to find a partner**. If you love a girl, you love their emotional storms, especially during their menstrual period or post-childbirth. It will be constant. It will all be on you.

I have seen people getting angry and throwing stuff in the house. Some people have killed their partners due to bad tempers. You need to show the full side of yourself when dating. You cannot change your partner's emotions, so you need to grow up and manage your own emotions.

You need some virtues called discipline and self-control. These virtues help you to overcome your tantrums and anger. If you still speak harshly to people in your anger, throw things at them and would not even speak to them, I suggest you wait until you have yourself under control before you say, 'Yes, I do!'

> *"Serving offers you the opportunity*
> *to demonstrate what you are made of,*
> *your character, humility and gifts."*

CHECKPOINT

FOR PARENTS

Which of the above attributes are you teaching your boys and girls before they leave home?

FOR YOURSELF

List the attributes you possess that confirm your maturity?

"Marriage will make someone your responsibility, duty or obligation to look after."

CHAPTER 6

Dependency in Relationship

"Very truly I tell you, when you were younger you dressed yourself and went where you wanted; but when you are old you will stretch out your hands, and someone else will dress you and lead you where you do not want to go."

- JOHN 21:8

"Great relationship has a bit of both dependency and independence. Too much dependency does not only scare them away, but it also kills love."

Great news! Everyone who wants to marry makes this claim. I am a big girl! I am a big boy! I am mature enough to make my own decisions. This is great! This is the expectation of parents and society that young people will grow and mature to make wise and good decisions. But maturity is not just what we say, but what we also do. The question is this, is there one size fits all for maturity? Are there levels of maturity?

You can measure the level of your maturity with three key indicators:

1. Your level of dependency
2. The level of your independence
3. The level of your interdependency

Let's dive in and take the meat!

> ***"No human being is perfect or self-sufficient in everything."***

Dependency is a state where one is limited in strength, knowledge or resources and hence needs the help of someone most of the time. No human being is perfect or self-sufficient in everything. You will need help, support, direction and even lifting when you are down. When you are infirm, you will need help from friends, nurses, doctors, parents and ultimately your partner.

When we are in any marital relationship, we have a degree of dependency on our spouse. You may depend on your spouse for food, clothing or money. Others depend on their spouses for protection and security at certain stages in their marriage. It is normal. **What is not normal in marriage is becoming a needy spouse all the time. It is not normal to want your spouse to do everything for you.**

DON'T BE A BIG BABY IF YOU WANT TO MARRY

Babies depend on their parents and family for everything until they grow up. No one expects children to wake up, brush their teeth, wash themselves and find food to eat. If your six-month-old baby woke up and began to do all that, the chance is that you may scream and probably run away.

Can you imagine, your one-month-old baby waking up in the morning and beginning to have a decent conversation with you, asking, *"Mum, how are you? Did you have a good sleep? Mum, what are we having for breakfast?"*

It is not their natural or default setting to do that. They are not expected to shower by themselves, dress up and say, *"Mum, I am going to look for a job."* We adults must do that for them. We must wash them, feed them, clothe them, and lift them up when they wake up. We gladly do that. It is because we know that in five years' time, they will begin to reduce their dependency on us and gradually move towards being independent. By the time they are 17-20 years old, we are expecting them to be about **90% independent** and **10% dependent.**

So, we understand that they will not be completely independent. No one is completely independent; all human beings have dependency needs.

BABY ADULTS ARE HIGH MAINTENANCE WHEN YOU MARRY THEM

Sadly, there are adults who are living like babies. They are too needy. It is all about them and what they will get from friends and family. They want people to look after them. They will not lift a finger on anything. They want people to wash their clothes, cook for them, give them money and even wipe their faces. They will not contribute to anything all by themselves. In fact, they have no mind of their own. They will not make any decisions without contacting their parents. **If you meet such persons, beware! They may be handsome, great-looking, and hold good qualifications, but if you have them as spouses, they will be high maintenance.** You can choose to marry them but be ready to be an engineer or a technician! You must fix everything for them!

If you are also a needy man or woman, with high dependency, it is probably better to wait before you ask anyone to marry you!

WHY ARE THEY SO NEEDY?

There are a few reasons that make people quite needy. Unfortunately, at this point, depending on their age and preparedness to change, it may stay with them for a long time, if not forever. This comes from the individual's upbringing and parenting that went wrong.

Overprotected children – Here they get attached to their parents. They are unable to transition into adulthood as quickly as expected. They are so fragile. They can't make decisions for themselves. This is because parents were not present to get them involved in anything in the house.

Spoilt children – May be due to single parenting, no parenting, or compensating parenting. Here children get what they want from their parents. Parents clean for them, iron for their teenage children, cook for them and even give them pocket money. Such children do not have to do anything at home. When they are in a relationship, they want to be treated the same way by their spouses. They are needy and want to be looked after.

Abusive family background – When children have been abused in the homes that are supposed to protect them, they become too scared. They crave protection all the time and in their marriage, they do the same.

Sara, 32, and a single mom of two tells her story.

"I come from a privileged family. My dad is a lawyer, and my mum is a doctor. I went to a private boarding school from age 10 until I completed A level. We had servants at home who did everything for me. I followed my parents to church because I had to satisfy them. My parents are both presbyters in our church, so I needed to behave as though I was a good girl. I graduated with a master's degree in Pharmacy. I knew I had to get married after school. But I was not sure what I needed to do because I never did anything for myself. I chose a boy my friends approved of but not my parents, but it did not bother me. After two years of dating, breakups and recovering several times, we finally made it to the altar. We both make good money but after four years of trying, we could not hold it together, the marriage was gone. I have realised that good families, good parents and good degrees do not guarantee successful marriages. I depended on my husband, Ben, to do the cooking, ironing and all the housework. In the end, he got fed up with me and left. If I had a second chance, I would learn to be more independent."

CHECKPOINT

FOR PARENTS

List five things you are teaching your boys at home to reduce their dependency before they finally leave.

List five things you are teaching your girls at home to reduce their dependency.

"What is not normal in marriage is becoming a needy spouse all the time."

CHAPTER 7

Independence in Relationship

"Independence from attachment is not necessarily a detachment from loving relationships but ending dependency."

Everyone strives to be independent. It is why we all groan to grow as fast as we can, so that we can attain the independence our parents and family have always denied us, albeit for our own good.

Children leaving home early these days means they learn to be independent early in life. This helps them to break the bonds and strongholds of parental control. It means they can pursue their God given gifts and develop their own skills and techniques away from their parents.

BREAKING PARENTAL CONTROL

Many young people living at home with their parents must always live their parents' lives. They do not feel they have their own lives. **Parents are wired to protect their offspring.** It is

something that comes naturally. They have fears they may lose their offspring; hence they lay hands on them tightly.

As they grow older, parents are supposed to expand their boundaries and territories and give children the freedom to choose and follow their own paths and dreams. Sadly, many parents fail to do this. This is the reason why many children rebel in many homes. This will have devastating effects when finally, children have opportunity to leave home. They want to go far away from them. They resent their parents. They will want to do what parents disagree with, just to prove they have their own minds and can do what they want. This usually happens when children move out and go to university. Let's listen to the pain Alice faces:

"My 18-year-old daughter, Carla, chose a university 350 miles away from our home. In fact, she never discussed her choices of university with me. I only saw it when her A-level results came. She rushed to me the morning she received her exams result. Luckily, she had 3 'A's and my husband and I were jumping for joy. She then told us, 'Parents I am going to Aberdeen university'. Her dad screamed, 'From Brighton all the way to Aberdeen. Are you crazy? This will not happen. You have two good universities around here. You must choose one of them'. Carla said, 'It is too late Dad. I want to leave you and your wife. I am tired of you both treating me like a child all the time. I need to grow. I need my freedom and independence'. I cried on the day she left. She will never call if we don't. She will find a job around the university. My heart is bleeding. But I realised we kept the boundaries too tight because she is an only child. We were overprotective. She did not like it. We did everything for her, thinking that it will make her happy. I

feel my husband and I have not been great parents. I feel we have ruined Carla's life, and I pray that God help her."

Carla went to the university in Aberdeen anyway because that was her first choice. At age 19, it is the first time she has left Brighton to go anywhere without her parents.

Carla says, *"Sadly, I am struggling at the university big time as I feel I lack social skills and awareness. I am afraid to be alone, but I think it is better than being at home with my controlling parents. Combining schoolwork and student life has been too challenging for me. Sometimes I cry all day in my room while my mates are out having fun. I thought I needed my independence, but I can see it is very expensive."*

INDEPENDENCE COMES AT A COST

This independence is supposed to prepare the youth for life in the world, including careers, living with others and forming relationships. It has, however, become a huge battleground for the devil to use to destroy family relationships. It has also become a huge battleground for psychological and mental conditions that affect both parents and children.

When the youth have bad mental health, their choices and perceptions are badly impacted. Youthful anxiety is now worse in Generation Z than any generation. They feel anxious, sick and lonely. Human beings are created to be social. *They crave friendship and community. When they don't find it, they substitute with internet games, sex, pornography, alcohol and drugs. They sink deeper into trouble after trouble.*

Some of these young people do not complete their university coursework or exams. **They are eventually booted out of**

university because they think independence means freedom to sleep, and not study. They think independence means to stop going to church. They think independence means to be promiscuous, cutting communication lines with their parents. They seek no parental or family support. Their parents will have no clue what these children are doing at university.

I have encountered children who have told parents they have completed university, but it turned out they never finished. Others finish with next to nothing grades. Some come out with huge debts. No one supervises their income and expenditure. They think student finance is great, but they end up overspending on fast food, drinks, alcohol and friends. This leaves them a huge mountain of debt.

MAKE YOUR INDEPENDENCE COUNT

Do not let your independence ruin your relationship with family and friends. Do not let your independence ruin your future and career. **Make sure your independence does not take you away from the church and God! On the contrary, make your time being independent the best time in your life where you are connecting, communicating and learning how to live with people besides your family.**

Let this time become a bridge to knowing God for yourself. Praying, worshipping and studying the word of God, as an independent youth preparing to be unleashed in service to God. Let this period be useful! This will have a great impact on how and whom you marry. When you are independent minded you will choose with counsel and prayer! *Marriage is great, but you must know that you will need your independence in choosing your spouse and being able to marry well.*

"They crave friendship and community. When they don't find it, they substitute with internet games, sex, pornography, alcohol and drugs. They sink deeper into trouble after trouble."

TO PARENTS: YOUR YOUTHS NEED ROOM

No one grows when they are in tight spaces. You need room to expand in knowledge, wisdom and understanding. You need room to develop your many God-given talents. You need room to wake up early as a youth to meet up with your God undisturbed. You need room to try your talent, hone them without feeling judged or insulted.

Matt says, "There is only one not-so – good university in our little town. I have also felt the buzz in bigger cities. I have plans to go to university in big cities and work there as well. Being the only child of my parents means that the idea of leaving to attend a university in another city terrifies them. Sometimes, I can hear my mom praying that I do not leave them, and that God should make me stay at home and attend the local university. I want to leave because I have become my mom's pet. She uses me against my dad. She wants to do everything for me. She does not leave me alone, neither does she give me any privacy."

They need room to learn to live with other people besides their own family. They need to wean off from the same community and influence. They need to see God for themselves. They need to pray for themselves. They need to stand up for themselves. They need room to apply what their parents have thought them. They need a place to compare notes.

Are the tools they have able to help them navigate the many troubles in this world? If not, what can they discard, learn and relearn to meet the demands of this current dispensation?

INDEPENDENCE BREEDS CONFIDENCE

Many young people are amazing at adapting to these challenges. Nothing scares them. They have an inbuilt capacity to adapt. Maybe due to their genetic or temperament makeup. Others have come from great families where parents have flexibility towards the children. They have timed their boundaries to perfection. Childhood and adolescence periods have been smoothly navigated without fallouts and drama. Children are at peace with family and themselves.

They are confident. Confident youths do not only know who they are, they also accept who they are. They choose what they want to do. They are not afraid to get it wrong. If they are from a Christian home, they have asked all difficult questions about God and religion. ***Parents have had time to explain to them, pray with them and fellowship with them. They don't go to church only when their parents are there.*** In fact, they take the lead in church service. They do their quiet time. They study the word independently. ***They are baptized, in both water, and in the Holy Ghost.***

They are independent in the things of God. They started serving in their local church. They will go to church, whether their parents are present or not. More about this when we come to spiritual qualification.

> ***"They are independent in the things of God."***

HOW DOES THIS AFFECT MARRIAGE?

In marriage, you will need a degree of independence to make this marriage work. You will need space and time to be who you are. ***You will need to be united with your spouse, but you***

must not lose your identity. Couples who have not learned to be independent in their relationship, seek separation as time goes on. It is because they have not given each other time and room to independently make decisions, seek God for themselves, or have their own time to be alone.

Independence does not also mean to be isolated from your spouse all the time. You married to be united with your spouse. You need to connect and engage with them. You need to form friendship with them. But you need to have a great balance between being friends, and being independent, to have a happy relationship.

CHECKPOINT

You can help to hasten your growth and independence. Please list three things you can do to hasten your growth and independence.

"Couples who have not learned to be independent in their relationship, seek separation as time goes on."

CHAPTER 8

Interdependency in Relationship

"The best relationship is one that does not foster too much independence nor too much dependence, but exist in the healthy interdependence zone."

KAREN SALMANSOHN

"As iron sharpens iron, so one person sharpens another."

PROVERBS 27:17 NIV

Society has taught us to be independent. So many individuals fight for their independence. They don't want to bother anyone, and they also don't want to be bothered. **There is a place for independence in your marriage, however, in marriage you cannot demand your independence all the time. This will ruin your relationship.** What you need more in your marriage is interdependency!

According to the author of 'Seven Habits of Highly Effective People', Stephen Covey, **interdependency is the highest growth**

of maturity. It sits on the apex. It is supreme. It is the boss of maturity. It is the king of maturity. Dependency has limitations. Independence has its limitations. **In fact, the real deal in any relationship is the capacity for interdependency.**

This will not only be needed in business and corporate setups, but they will also be essential requirements in a long-lasting relationship. **You cannot marry successfully without the capacity for interdependency.**

All people wanting to marry must aspire to be at this level. Unfortunately, you cannot rush interdependence. It is a process. You must desire. You must be patient. You must thirst for it.

WHAT IS INTERDEPENDENCY?

This is the quality of being able to support each other for survival, accomplishment and performance within a group of individuals, such as marriage and family. In marriage, couples support each other in prayer, trauma, troubles, financially and emotionally.

The writer of Proverbs puts it this way:

> *"As iron sharpens iron,*
> *so one person sharpens another."*
> PROVERBS 27:17 NIV

Cathy and David shared their story of interdependency:

"It seems we were made for each other. Where I am weak, David is stronger. He complements me so well that our marriage is thriving every day. I don't like cooking, but David loves it. David doesn't like ironing and washing up, but these are my favourite, is this not weird? We depend on each other for mutual satisfaction and

protection. But I think the reason is simple, our backgrounds are similar. We both come from bigger families. Chores were shared at home, and everyone must be involved. My siblings were naughty and annoying, but they have helped me cope with anyone I meet. I am now reaping the benefits in my marriage even after 12 years in marriage."

Couples must take pains to climb up from dependency through independence, and climax at interdependency. It is at this point where cooperation, teamwork, friendship, honesty, sharing and sharing ideas enable couples to live in harmony and build a strong lasting relationship.

Interdependence is so critical that if a person is not able to achieve it, they will be better off remaining single, continuing to redo their homework until they have passed with flying colours BEFORE they consider dating or marriage. In interdependence, you are not asking what your spouse can do for you, you are finding a way of doing things together for the benefit of everyone. You are looking to work together for maximum benefits.

"Couples must take pains to climb up from dependency through independence,and climax at interdependency."

NO EXCUSES! INTERDEPENDENCY EVERYWHERE

> *"Now if the foot should say, "Because I am not a hand, I do not belong to the body," it would not for that reason stop being part of the body. And if the ear should say, "Because I am not an eye, I do not belong to the body," it would not for that reason stop being part of the body. If the whole body were an eye, where would the sense of hearing be? If the whole body were an ear,*

> *where would the sense of smell be? But in fact God has placed the parts in the body, every one of them, just as he wanted them to be."*
>
> 1 CORINTHIANS 12:15-18 NIV

If you were thinking that you are not married, you don't live with parents or family and that you are handicapped, think again. God has made provision for you to learn wherever you are. Even in spiritual gifts, there is interdependence as Paul stated in 1 Corinthians 12 above.

INTERDEPEND WITH PEOPLE AROUND YOU

Please note that one of the drawbacks of remaining independent is difficulty in living with other people. Christ said, *"In as much as it depends on you, live at peace with all men."* – Romans 12:18

This means that all people living under this sun must in one way or another live with their fellow men. You may not like some people and would like to avoid their company at all costs, but there are people you haven't got that choice to make about. You will have to live or work with them.

These people include your parents, siblings, friends, work colleagues, students, teachers and even your enemies. In fact, they are a means of helping you achieve interdependence. They will depend on you for many things. You also depend on them. **They will come in so many shapes and sizes. They have different mindsets. They have different perceptions. They have different tastes. They have different behaviours. It may seem strange that they are not like you.** But it is normal. This is how you appreciate individuality and their differences. Some are able but some are disabled. We are all not the same. But we have different skill sets that someone needs at different times.

God is so wise. He is an intelligent designer. He knows the heart of men. You see, there is no man on earth who has it all. You lack so many things as a person. What you don't have, someone else has. So, you need them to support you. The skills and abilities you have will be useless if there is none to benefit from you.

In your family home, you will see that some people are better doing certain tasks than you. Some are cleverer than you. Some have abilities you will never have. Your gender means you can do certain tasks better or less than your opposite gender.

The intelligent God also created us with inherent desire for warmth, acceptance and affection. That means you will always need people in your life to talk to, hold you and even cuddle you. There are certain times and seasons, you feel like you can be so independent you do not need anyone. But there comes another season you may have money, a car, a house and everything, yet you miss the companionship of fellow human beings. You do not operate as an island. To be able to live with fellow human beings you will have to cooperate with them. Usually, this is the reason many people seek to marry.

> ***"That means you will always need people in your life to talk to, hold you and even cuddle you."***

INTERDEPENDENCE IS TEAMWORK

I like what a Ghanaian marriage counsellor and marriage speaker, Elder Kevin Annan, says about "**TEAM**". He says the acronym is "together everyone achieves more". You can be the one with the best brain, but the effort of two or more people together is far bigger than a single person. Some of you pray a lot alone. It is great, but you are missing out on the power of team prayer. God endorsed this:

> *"Then the Lord said, 'If as one people speaking the same language, they have begun to do this, then nothing they plan to do will be impossible for them.'"*
>
> GENESIS 11:6 NIV

> *"Again, truly I tell you that if two of you on earth agree about anything they ask for, it will be done for them by my Father in heaven. For where two or three gather in my name, there am I with them."*
>
> MATTHEW 18:19-20 NIV

Interdependence says team up to pray! Team up to bring up the children. Team up to fight and conquer.

AGREEMENT AND COOPERATION

Can two walk together unless there is agreement? ***If agreement and cooperation are big indicators of maturity, selfishness is a bigger indicator of immaturity.*** If you are still protecting what you have, failing to share, and struggling to live with others, it is time to work on yourself to become interdependent.

One of the greatest assets of a couple is their power to achieve more. A couple who fails to realise the enormity of grace and power within them as a team, miss out big time.

To be married means that you agree to join and work together as one mighty force with your spouse. You must be ready to enrol with them to work together. If you are not ready to be interdependent, please seek not to be united with a human being. Don't marry!

James and Jane have been married for five years and are blessed with two kids. James says, "Before marriage, we were constantly praying together on the phone, in the park and even on the street. But as soon as we got married Jane, would never be ready for prayer. She will always have a reason not to pray with me. This has seriously affected our relationship. We are not united. We face a barrage of attacks every day, and I feel powerless."

If you are ready to work with someone to achieve more, get ready to marry. If you are, however, someone who wants to be independent all the time, maybe it is not the right time for you to marry.

> ***"One of the greatest assets of a couple is their power to achieve more."***

HOW TO ASCEND INTERDEPENDENCE

A few ways to reach the apex of interdependence:

1. Show interest in people you live with and those you meet at church, workplace and everywhere.
2. Learn to share what you have. Be generous. It is a mark of unselfishness.
3. Learn to serve people rather than expecting to be served.
4. Develop your communication skills to be able to interact with people.
5. Always check around for what you can do, even when no one is watching or telling you what to do.
6. Accept that you will never be all sufficient. You should welcome correction and guidance from experienced people.

7. God has placed desire for community in you. You will crave for company.
8. Treat everyone as special and unique regardless of their physical appearance.
9. Be prepared to offer help. In return, good measure, pressed down, shaken together, will men put into your bosom.
10. Love attracts love. Show people love and they will return love. Be mean and they will do same to you.
11. Forgive. Accept that you are not an angel. People forgive you all the time.
12. Be kind and patient towards others. Understand that we don't all have same abilities.
13. Teamwork. Be eager to work with people. Two heads are better than one.
14. Appreciate other people's gifts and talents. If you do, they will do the same to you.
15. Be honest with people. If you are honest with them, you will be honest with your spouse. You will reap the benefits thereof.

Paul, 27, and an usher in the local church says, "My parents are not together. I did not see my dad until I was 18 when I was going to university. My mom brought up three of us single handedly. But we were determined we will not let this deter us from achieving our dreams. My mom is my rock. She is my go-to person. She brought us up with church, prayer and the fear of God. I serve my family with joy. And I serve my church not just being an usher but also helping to set up for church and unpacking. The church is my spiritual home. My fiancée does the same thing. Her parents allow her the freedom to serve in the church Bible study team and as a singer. We are both graduates. We are working and earning decent wages as we prepare to marry next month."

Paul's mom says, "I introduced my kids to Christ and trusted that they will always do the right thing. As a single mom, I know I am not always home to supervise them. But I trusted their faith in God will see them through. They have been trained in all domestic chores. They look after me and I look after them. I have no doubt in my mind that that Paul will be a great husband and father."

If your parents or any member of your family can vouch for you like Paul's mom, you know you are on course for a good marriage because you have been trained well.

CHECKPOINT

How much time do you contribute to helping at home independently without your parents asking?

Please list five tasks you undertake at your parents' home independently.

ONE FOR THE BOYS

Many cultures treat boys as princes. Parents do not ask them to clean or cook. The boys have so much time to do whatever they want. They seem to have total independence. They hide in their rooms, doing God knows what.

If you are privileged to be in this category, do you think it is fair that your old man, mother and sister are doing all house chores whilst you hide in your room? When you get married, your wife will not do everything for you. How will you manage the home without becoming a needy husband?

GUIDE TO CHORES

Don't forget the following chores. Please check and initial to confirm that you are good to go:

Chore	Check	Initials
Making jollof rice		
Seasoning chicken		
Peeling yams		
Frying eggs		
Drying clothes		
Cleaning fridges		
Cleaning the toilet bowl		
Cleaning the bath		
Checking on family members		
Praying		
Studying the Bible		
Washing cars		
Gardening		
Simple do it yourself (Diy)		
Ironing clothes		
Food shopping		
Cooking pasta		
Replacing light bulbs		
Using the washing machine		

 **CHECKPOINT**

Boys, list three things you need to learn or polish in the next 4 weeks.

ONE FOR THE GIRLS

How much help do you offer your parents at home? If your parents were not available today, do you know where everything is? Will the house be clean? Will you cook any food? If you have younger siblings, how much attention do you pay to their training? I know in many homes, you do it all. You are well trained and ready for your would-be husband. I am also aware that some of you girls babysit your brothers, even those older than you. You wash their clothes, and iron for them. You do all the cooking and fetch the food for them in their room. You shield and insulate them from house chores.

How much are you contributing to their dependency or independence? I know it is not your responsibility to train them, but you become complicit with their high dependency and immaturity.

GUIDE TO CHORES

Please read and confirm which of the following chores you are competent at doing:

Chore	Check	Initials
Making jollof rice		
Seasoning chicken		
Peeling yams		
Frying eggs		
Drying clothes		
Cleaning fridges		
Cleaning the toilet bowl		
Cleaning the bath		
Checking on family members		
Praying		
Studying the Bible		
Washing cars		
Gardening		
Simple do it yourself (DIY)		
Ironing clothes		
Food shopping		
Cooking pasta		
Replacing light bulbs		
Using the washing machine		

 CHECKPOINT

Girls, list three things you think you need to polish before you graduate from your parent's home.

IN CONCLUSION

Marriage is fun for those who prepare well. Those who are intentional about learning the art of living, growing and maturing into adulthood. Those who have marriage in sight and painstakingly work hard to be interdependent. Such people should be encouraged to marry. Those who have not made any effort to move from dependency, at the foot of the ladder to independence, and perch at the apex of the ladder of interdependence should never be given any encouragement to marry.

> *"Dependency has limitations.*
> *Independence has its limitations."*

CHAPTER 9

Maturity to Live With People

"If it is possible, as far as it depends on you, live at peace with everyone."

ROMANS 12:18 NIV

God the Almighty, all-knowing and all-present, did not like to be alone. It is the reason we have the Triune God. Therefore, in God, we have God the Father, the Son and the Holy Spirit. They live together and function well with each other.

As if that was not enough, God created man and put him in the Garden of Eden. Why? So that from time to time He would visit man and have a chat. God enjoys 'relationship' with the Trinity, with each other, and with man.

> *"And they heard the sound of the LORD God walking in the garden in the cool of the day, and Adam and his wife hid themselves from the presence of the LORD God among the trees of the garden."*
>
> GENESIS 3:8 NKJV

You should understand this, it is not in the interest of God for man to live alone. When God created man, he put something in us, which is His nature that makes us desire to be with people. We become insufficient and lonely if we have no one to speak to or be around.

When we are detached from God and people it is impossible to survive or be sane. But herein lies the question? How long can we go without each other? Then again, when we are with people, how long should we be with them? When do we begin to feel we need a break from them? And in the case of marriage, is it not daunting to live with the same person for the rest of your life?

You see, God desires an everlasting relationship with man just as he has with the Son and the Holy Ghost. The very same desire is in man. We all need our friends, our families and our spouses. As human beings, we are better with other people. But make no mistake, God did not find it easy to live with man permanently. You will also not find it easy to live with any man.

> *"When God created man,*
> *he put something in us,*
> *which is His nature that makes*
> *us desire to be with people."*

WHY IS IT SO DIFFICULT TO LIVE WITH PEOPLE?

There are several reasons why this happens:

Created Differently

We are not created the same. We have minds of our own and we do not think the same.

Different Personalities

We also have different personalities given to us by God so that we can fulfil our individual divine assignments. Do not expect your friend or your spouse to be the same as you.

Different Temperaments

Some people are introverted while others are extroverted. That means we react to things differently. Our visions and perceptions are different. It is important to understand that the person you are going to marry will not be the same as you. Because of the drive, desire and destiny that God has placed in us, we act and behave differently. This is normal and you should not be surprised.

Background

We are also shaped by our background. Your family of origin, parents and the setting you grew up with will influence your thoughts, understanding and perception. If by God's grace, you leave your family homes, you will still be exposed to many more varieties in behaviour and perceptions.

Education

This includes what type of education or training you receive, which will also affect your behaviour and perception.

Religious Beliefs

Beliefs affect your thinking and behaviour. As a Christian you are expected to repent and follow Christ's teachings. These teachings might be different from what you have been taught, trained, or practised. Sometimes you must unlearn or relearn what you know. Even two Christian couples may have problems.

THEY WILL NEVER BE YOU AND YOU WILL NEVER BE THEM

When you are being critical or judgmental, you should remember that it is not all your partner's fault:

- You wish they could be as active, proactive and discerning as you.
- You wish they were as smart as you.
- You wish they were as eloquent and great communicators as you.
- You wish they were as patient as you.
- You are unique and so are they.

But I am afraid they will not be like you. You are not going to marry another you.

"As human beings, we are better with other people."

YOUR PARTNER WAS NOT CREATED FOR YOU ALONE

Your spouse was not created for you alone. You might not like his slowness, his perceived lack of enthusiasm and his too-outgoing personality. But God did that for a reason and a purpose. Some people are eagerly waiting for his patience and how he takes his time to answer everybody. Some companies are headhunting him. He is a great asset with all those qualities.

Don't change them. Adapt to them! Now that you are aware you can't change anyone, what do you have to do? It is time to find ways of having a peaceful coexistence with people. Time to accept who everyone is. It is time to lower your expectations. It is time to understand that other people are accepting you the way you are. Your boyfriend or girlfriend has been kind to you because he or she loves you.

Close your eyes. The reason why you can see too many faults of him or her is because you are blind to his or her good deeds. Your spouse does 100 things freely for you. She or he makes only one mistake, and that is what you are dwelling on.

Why don't you open your eyes to find and acknowledge the many great things they do for you for free and appreciate them? You will do yourself a big service if you close your ears and eyes to their tiny, few and harmless mistakes. After all, you also make mistakes. Close your eyes and ears and allow your spouse to learn from his or her own experiences.

 CHECKPOINT

SELF-ASSESSMENT TEST

Reason I Want to Marry	Yes	No
Am I old enough to marry? 20+		
Am I mature to handle the pressure of living with a stranger?		
Do I cope with living with my siblings and parents?		
Do I want an escape route from my family home?		
Do I want to marry because all my friends are getting married?		
Do I know what husband and wife do in marriage?		
Have I gotten my education sorted to an appreciable level?		

Is my career also sorted?		
Have I prepared financially?		
Am I convinced of this person I want to marry?		
Can I trust him/her to spend the rest of my life with?		
Do our parents agree to our getting married?		
Do we both have the same faith?		
Do I genuinely love this person?		

Reason Why I Want to Marry	Yes	No
Are you convinced of this person you want to marry?		
Do you know more about his/her background?		
Is he/she not going out with any other person?		
Do you think he/she will meet all the socio-economic-emotional-spiritual needs?		
Is this person kind and forgiving?		
Has he/she got respect for parents and other people?		
Is this person matured spiritually and emotionally?		

"Don't change them. Adapt to them!"

SECTION THREE

LOVE IS A MATTER OF CHOICE

CHAPTER 10

Your Keys to Right Choices

"But if serving the Lord seems undesirable to you, then choose for yourselves this day whom you will serve, whether the gods your ancestors served beyond the Euphrates, or the gods of the Amorites, in whose land you are living. But as for me and my household, we will serve the Lord."

JOSHUA 24:15 NIV

"Choice is not only a place, it is also a junction. At this junction, if you take the right turn, you reach your correct and desired destination. Take the wrong turn and you miss your destination and destiny."

Welcome to Choice! A place where lives are changed, and destinies are defined. You will define your future with whosoever you choose to date or marry! No one will do that for you. It is your gift from God to make your own choice.

This is what God, through Joshua, said to the people of Israel, that they must choose! We choose every day. Whether it is going to school or not. Whether to buy a house or not. We also choose whether to marry or not and who we want to marry.

You should be intentional about your choice. Choice is not luck. It is not a game. It is a matter of life and death! It is the exercise of your choice that defines whether you will be happy in marriage or not. *It is your power. It is your God-given gift. Use your choice but use it wisely.* Where there is a choice, there are alternatives. You have almost 8 billion people on earth to choose one person to marry.

But all you need is one gentle soul, kind-hearted, honest, beautiful in your own eyes, a mature and God-fearing person! One who loves and adores you! One who will feel your heart beating each morning. It is that simple!

But it is all about you. You are the most important subject here! Because you must choose! It is simple but not straight forward!

> ***"You should be intentional about your choice."***

THE PROBLEM OF CHOICE

Choice is one of the biggest problems you will face daily in your life. When you have two or more possibilities to select from, you must be careful to select not just the best, but which is right and suitable for you.

God did not give Adam the best woman. He gave him a suitable woman. She was beautiful in Adam's own eyes! But in our dispensation, you have the power to choose and present them to God for blessing in church.

What will you consider before you make your choice? Would the person you choose also choose you back? Just remember, although choice is free, it is not without cost and consequences. There is a price to pay for each choice.

CONSEQUENCES OF CHOICE

You are right, or wrong.
You are happy, or unhappy.
You get criticised or you get credited.
You pass, or you fail.
You become sane, or insane.
You will be a victim, or victorious.

The list can go on and on...

To live happily ever after depends on your CHOICE, the person you choose to be your husband or wife. I don't want to scare you, but there are far too many men and women whose lives have ended miserably, due to bad choices. There are far too many people who have lost their capacity to think straight. Some of them are borderline insane, whilst others are insane.

There are too many people leaving their marriage within one to seven years of marriage. The two reasons I hear all the time are, "*He or she is not good for me*" or "*I did not take my time to make the right choice.*" The purpose of this section is to help you avoid this costly mistake which many people your age make most of the time.

> *"To live happily ever after depends on your CHOICE, the person you choose to be your husband or wife."*

FIVE UNMISSABLE KEYS TO THE RIGHT CHOICES

How can I avoid the mistakes that are putting others into mental homes? There are five important things I feel should guide you in making the right choices.

1. Prayer

Every believer seeking a partner must pray to God to help them make the right choices. ***Prayer may not deliver a wife into your bedroom in our dispensation as He did for Adam, but prayer will bring illumination and conviction.*** I hear some believers and men of God claiming that they prayed, and God gave them their spouses. Fair enough, God can do all things. However, it is very difficult for anyone to validate these claims. Sadly, these same people of God divorce the spouses they claim God gave them.

My counsel is this, when you have prayed, act on it and God will lead you as he did for the servant of Abraham:

> *"For the Lord, the God of heaven, who took me from my father's house and my native land, solemnly promised to give this land to my descendants. He will send his angel ahead of you, and he will see to it that you find a wife there for my son."*
>
> GENESIS 24:7 NLT

Abraham then sends the Chief servant on his way. With obedience, humility and faith, listen to the prayer of the servant:

> *"'12 Lord, God of my master, Abraham,' he prayed. 'Please give me success today, and show unfailing love to my master, Abraham. 13 See, I am standing here beside this spring, and the young women of the town*

> *are coming out to draw water.* [14] *This is my request. I will ask one of them, 'Please give me a drink from your jug.' If she says, 'Yes, have a drink, and I will water your camels, too!'—let her be the one you have selected as Isaac's wife. This is how I will know that you have shown unfailing love to my master.' Before he had finished praying, he saw a young woman named Rebekah coming out with her water jug on her shoulder. She was the daughter of Bethuel, who was the son of Abraham's brother Nahor and his wife, Milcah.*
> [16] *Rebekah was very beautiful and old enough to be married, but she was still a virgin. She went down to the spring, filled her jug, and came up again."*
>
> GENESIS 24:12-16 NLT

This is the one vivid account recorded in the Bible, showing us how Abraham prayed for a wife for his son. Abraham and his servant joined their faith together to pray for a wife for Isaac. God heard them. God responded immediately. A precedence has been set. You can also join your faith with someone, a friend or family, and pray for a spouse. In prayer, God can give direction on what steps you need to take. He can also shine your eyes on one person who would be your spouse.

Prayer can also enable you to respect the guidance of your parents and other mature people. But be warned that this does not mean that you must select your wife in the same way as Abraham did for Isaac. After all, fetching water from spring is rare in many places. You can pray for your own signs as proof.

The servant did not complicate things when he was proposing to Rebecca. He did not say, "*The spirit of God has revealed to me that you are Isaac's wife!"* Or *"That sayeth the Lord, you will be a good wife for my master's son!"*

Young men, you don't need to propose to your lady by saying, *"That sayeth the Lord"*. I do not also encourage young women to do that. You should not propose to anyone by alluding to God. If you have a conviction in your spirit, say, *"I have prayed, and I am convinced that we can be a good couple."* or *"If you agree to marry me, we shall build a fantastic life together."*

You must always give them the chance to also pray and be convinced. Please don't shut people up with claims from God that no one can verify.

2. Discerning

Discerning is your ability to distinguish the good from the bad. The ability to distinguish the genuine from the fake. It is your capacity to see beyond natural visibility. A third eye to see the lies and insincerity. It is also that third eye to see the hidden truth of this person.

It is also the ability to distinguish someone with great potential from those with lesser potential. It is the capacity to see into the future beyond what is presented now. *Maybe their present qualification is lower, but you can smell a PhD all around them. Their bank balance may not attract you, but you have the eye to see millions of pounds around them. These are the Josephs, Daniels and Davids.* When they propose to you, can you discern the future with them?

If you found Joseph in the pit, would you marry him? Would you be able to see that he was a future Prime Minister of Egypt? This is what every believer should pray for. The grace to see beyond the present! The ability to detect those who lie to you. False pretenders. Those who just want to use you today because of what you have or what they need from you. Watch out.

Pray for discernment! This is also a gift from God! Men and women who want to have a happy and successful marriage need to ask God to open their eyes!

I met a man of God who was going through a difficult time with his wife of one year, "I blame myself. I should have known better. I have fallen into the devil's trap. In fact, I have married the daughter of the devil himself."

This is exactly what he said. Is this not sad to hear this coming from the mouth of a man of God? You should not let this happen to you.

To do that, you need to do the following:

- Wait on God for direction
- Let God shine his light on any area which is hidden
- Reduce your fun and excitement and be serious
- Listen to your heart if you're prayerful
- Be a good judge of character and behaviour

> ***"Discerning is your ability to distinguish the good from the bad. Ability to distinguish the genuine from the fake."***

3. Due Diligence

This is the ability to search and research who this person is and what his or her motives are. This is like discerning, but this is a more physical and emotional search. You want to ask friends, family and associates how they see this person.

Are they what they say they really are? Should I take them by their word? You cannot marry people based on what they say alone. You must find the means to validate what they say before you give them your heart, especially the ladies. *Ensure the content matches what is written on the tin.*

This is a serious matter before you. Do not start celebrating because he is the PENSA president who says he loves you. Don't start celebrating because a person you met on Instagram says they love you. Ask yourself this question. Do they pretend to love me because of what they will profit from me? Do they love me because I am vulnerable? This is where your intuition, heart feeling, and comments from well-wishers come in handy.

Do you listen or are you blinded by love? When people are blinded by love, they do not ask questions because they fear they will lose this person. When you are desperate, you will not listen to your heart. Even if your heart says, "Don't do it, this person is not good for you." You will give yourself all kinds of excuses, and you will do it. Friends and family will warn you, but you will ignore every advice and sheepishly follow this person.

Andy, 35, a civil engineer says, "I met Demi on Instagram 2 years ago. She was so beautiful. I decided to pursue her. We started talking. Some of her stories did not add up, but I did not pay attention to them. I just wanted her. She was in Leeds, and I was in London. I visited her a couple of times and we decided to tell our churches to arrange for marriage within six months of dating. She revealed to me that she did not have the right to stay in the UK but that was okay with me. We got married anyway. It was a beautiful wedding. Her mother and father flew from Nigeria to attend the wedding. But two months after the wedding, I discovered what turned out to be heart-breaking secrets. Not only did she not have a womb, in fact she had two children in Nigeria. She was also in credit card debt of £25,000 that the bailiffs were chasing her. This catalogue of lies made me feel sick. The love and the feeling I had for her just disappeared from me. I filed for divorce straight away. But instead of blaming Demi, I blame myself for lack of checks and the speed in which I married her."

Every person going through divorce tells me the same thing all the time. Especially those whose marriage lasted for a short time. "*I saw all the red flags, but I ignored them, hoping that they would change or would never happen.*" People do not change that quickly, and you cannot change them either. If you see anything that is a secret, or a lie, the chance is that there are more secrets and lies you don't know. ***They say that lies are like rats, when you see one, the chance is that there are a thousand of them hiding that you don't see.***

> ***"People do not change that quickly, and you cannot change them either."***

4. Dreams and Visions

God has constantly revealed Himself to His people through visions and dreams. The Holy Spirit has done that over the years. Many Christians take their dreams and visions very seriously. This is because they have observed that God speaks to them through dreams and visions. You need to learn how God speaks to you in all matters, not just when you want to choose a person to marry. If God speaks to you or reveals a person you need to marry through supernatural means, that is great! It makes your job easier. However, it is important to wait and seek confirmation from the person or from other sources.

Jane 29 says, "My dreams and visions are very accurate in most cases, especially those when I wake up in the morning and I can recount them vividly. One week before Elijah proposed to me, I saw everything in my dream. He had met me in town and said, 'Jane, it is lunchtime, do you want to join me for lunch over there?' and pointed to a restaurant opposite. Whilst we were eating and having a conversation, it felt so good to be around him. I imagined being with him as a husband. Then toward the end, he asked me if I could be his girlfriend. But I did not have the chance to reply, and my eyes were opened. I was so angry the following morning for the missed opportunity. But I started praying over this. One week after this, I was in town and met Elijah at the same spot. I was freaking out. This was weird. Then he asked me out at the same restaurant. And towards the end, he asked me if I did not have anyone in my life, would I consider to be his girlfriend? I looked at him and I was smiling. Then I said, 'This is crazy, but my answer is yes!'"

Be careful you do not go to this sister or brother and say, "*I was in the spirit, and in a vision, I saw you presented to me as a wife or husband.*" Choosing a spouse is not the end, it is the effort and the work you put in to make the marriage work that matters to God. God created all sorts of people on earth. God is interested in the life of everyone. You should only choose a spouse after prayerful consideration.

Over-spiritualisation of choice can be very confusing for young believers, especially when pastors and church leaders stand on the podium to make such pronouncements. Younger believers and followers who want to marry then want to see the same visions or dreams before they say 'yes'. **Let me be clear that there is nowhere in the scriptures that we have such examples, and**

we have also not been prescribed such formulae to follow anywhere in the Bible.

However, dreams and visions are all means God communicates with his children.

5. The Peace of Mind from God

Prophecies, dreams, revelations and visions are all means that God speak to Christians. They make you feel good and very much assured when you receive them. But don't ignore that calmness, comfort and assurance you experience when you are with this person. This is the peace of God that guides your heart and mind. Peace of mind that follows the confidence in your choice. You should be happy and free in your spirit when you say yes. You should be doubtless and fearless, as there is no fear in love. When you begin to fear, sit back, reflect and pray!

> *"Then you will experience God's peace,*
> *which exceeds anything we can understand.*
> *His peace will guard your hearts and minds*
> *as you live in Christ Jesus."*
>
> PHILIPPIANS 4:7 NLT

Rita 30-year-old nurse and single told me this, "When I informed my church leaders of the man I want to marry, there was a barrage of questions that made me doubt my own choice. Have you heard from God? Do you think he is the one? Why are you so sure this is the man for you?"

Rita almost in tears said, "Papa, please show me, how did you choose Auntie Amma? How did you hear from God? I am confused because there seems to be a particular way that I need to hear from God, either in dreams or in visions."

Rita was very surprised when I said, "I cannot say for certain that God asked me to marry my wife. I said, as a praying man, I have desires, and I also have a choice. God respects my choice that gives me the peace of mind."

Your choice or acceptance of this person's proposal if you are a prayerful person, will fill your heart with inexplicable joy. Your friends, family, mentors and spiritual leaders will confirm you have a good deal!

Moses, 27, said, "I have long admired Helen, but I thought it was just infatuation. But any time I see her in church or even outside the church, my heart starts beating. She is so attractive to me, and I feel we will make a great couple. But I was so scared to approach her because I have not had any dreams and visions about her. But when I discussed this with my mom, she assured me it would be fine to make a move. I asked her out for coffee in town. Even before I requested if it was alright to be together, I could not look her in the face. She was so beautiful, and I could not believe she was single. I wore a hoody, because I was so scared she would say no. And she did! I wanted the earth to break open for me to disappear! As I pulled the hoody to cover my face, she held my hand softly and said, 'I have been waiting for this moment with you for a long time, but are you sure of what you just said? Tell me why you want to be with me. Have you prayed over this?' I waffled a little bit, and I said, 'I have prayed a lot about you. I am sure you and I will make a good couple if you would give it a chance'. Then she stood up and drew me to herself and said, yes! This was the best moment of my life. For the next 24 months, the peace that I felt within my heart was unimaginable. We are now married with one child, and I am glad I did it."

So, you can see that Moses and Helen did not have visions, but they were at peace with each other. This is also the work of God. Our God is not a one-way God.

CHECKPOINT

If you have a boyfriend or a girlfriend, please list 3 things that helped you settle on this person:

"Your choice or acceptance of this person's proposals if you are a prayerful person, will fill your heart with inexplicable joy."

CHAPTER 11

Your Desires and Preferences

"For it is God who works in you to will and to act in order to fulfil his good purpose."

PHILIPPIANS 2:13 NIV

"Every person has inner desires and cravings that should never be ignored. These desires or wishes are the marks of what you can tolerate and what you cannot."

Human beings have an inner craving to connect with someone. But beware that living with any human being is hard. This is due to other inner vices we all struggle with to shift away. We are incredibly selfish as human beings. It is part of our DNA. We are also arrogant and proud by nature. Above all, none of us is fully adequate. We are simply inadequate in all things even if we feel we know it all, we don't.

So naturally, when we want to choose a spouse, we want someone who is pure and unselfish, one who is kind and gentle even though we are not. But men and women are different. That is another reason why marriage is hard. Then you also must understand the growth and changes that will happen along the way. How much are you prepared to cope with them? God wants everyone he created to do well. But based on your background and training, you will tolerate some characters more than others. It also depends on your motivation to marry. **Your choice will be influenced by your desires and priorities.**

Sadly, many people enter marriage without any expectations apart from sex. They did not know what to expect from this husband or wife. All their mates were married, so they also got married! They have never read any marriage books. They never knew there were marriage requirements, and what they were!

The things that are likely to influence your choice could be: physical appeal, spiritual appeal or even psychological appeal. But you should know what makes you fall in love with that person!

> *"Human beings have an inner craving to connect with someone."*

DEFINING YOUR PREFERENCES: SETTING YOUR PRIORITIES RIGHT!

Your desires or wishes are the marks of what you can tolerate and what you cannot. It is the Lord who has filled our hearts with this. Let's see how Paul puts it:

> *"For it is God who works in you to will*
> *and to act in order to fulfil his good purpose."*
>
> PHILIPPIANS 2:13

I do not mean your ungodly lust and passion. But I am expecting that as a praying and holy believer, you have good desires in your heart. Without these desires and attractions, you will run after every human being and marry them. These desires can be both physical and spiritual. Translated into modern language, it is called attraction. You will be attracted to a man or a woman with certain inherent or physical qualities.

When you love someone romantically, there is something about them that attracts you. Jesus' love is free. It is unconditional. Human beings will always love you for a reason. **God will not judge you for defining what you want from a man or a woman you want to marry. He will rather judge you for making a careless choice and not honouring your vow.**

Sara, 25, and recent Cambridge University graduate says, "I am educated to master's degree level so the man I want to marry must be at least a degree holder, educated in Europe or America. I am 5.6 ft so I want a man who is at least 6.0 feet tall. A man who is friendly with a sense of humour is attractive to me. I want our children to look good, so I want a man who is good looking, who wants to exercise with me. This sounds a bit carnal, but in my heart, I want a man who is hairy and to have a groomed beard. This man must be in the house of God always. He is a praying man, tongue speaking and helpful at church. I don't care about money, but I want him to be hardworking and ambitious."

The truth is simple. If you don't ask you don't get! It is said that if you don't know where you are going, every point you reach can be a destination. In much the same way, if you don't know what you want you may choose anyone you want, but it can be a source of pain in your heart later. ***If you don't know what you want from a spouse, the chance is that it is not the right time to choose to date.***

"The truth is simple. If you don't ask you don't get."

BOYS' AND GIRLS' ZONES – MIX AND MATCH FOR YOUR FUTURE PARTNER

People you want to marry come in different shapes and sizes. They have different qualifications, virtues and vices. There are certain behaviours and characters you will never detect until after marriage. But some of them will be visible just on your first date.

But if you are vigilant, many behaviours will also be seen, either at the beginning, or in the middle of the relationship. A lot of them will be so subtle they will require microscopic mind and eyes to detect.

> *"If you fall asleep at the time of dating, you should blame yourself if you open your eyes and find yourself in the wrong destination after the wedding."*

ACTIVITY – LOVE WISH LIST

Your task today is to select the qualities you expect in your potential spouse. You have four sections to select up to **20 qualities** from. Physical appearance, Profession, Spiritual, Attitude or Character. Try to pick 5 from each section.

Physical Appearance

- Short
- Tall
- Average height for male
- Average height for female
- Big hips
- Big buttocks
- Long hair
- Short hair
- Fair colour
- Dark colour

- Big calves
- Big breasts
- No colour option
- Afro-hair
- Blonde
- Brunette
- Big person
- Small person
- Neat
- Tidy
- Ugly
- Unattractive
- Untidy
- Small legs
- Big head
- Small head
- Small eyes
- Big eyes
- Big nose
- Small nose
- Gentleman
- Lady

Profession

- Rich
- Employed
- Direct career pathway
- Business-oriented person
- Unemployed
- Job seeker
- On benefit
- No decent job
- Apprentice
- Student
- Business owner
- Self-employed
- Part-time job
- Tradesman
- Education
- PhD
- Masters
- First degree
- Diploma
- Certificate
- A level
- High school
- Primary
- No education
- Can read
- Can write

Spiritual

- Christian
- Church goer
- Prayerful
- Serious Christian
- Spiritual
- Zealous for Christ
- Matured Christian
- Bible believing
- Tongue speaking
- Bible-based person
- Knows the word
- Too busy to pray
- Doesn't believe in long prayer
- No quiet time
- Doesn't believe spending long time at church
- Doesn't get involved in church except on Sundays

Attitude or Character

- Gentleman
- Kind
- Respect for adults
- Respect for women
- Generous
- Caring
- Sharing
- Funny
- Abusive
- Humble
- Soft spoken
- Assertive
- Firm
- Wise
- Intelligent
- Knowledgeable
- Forgiving
- Welcoming
- Hospitable
- Teachable
- Resilient
- Focus
- Serious
- Hardworking
- Protective
- Loving
- Warm
- Considerate
- Confident
- Neat
- Articulate
- Supportive

- Sympathetic
- Bad temperament
- Quick temper
- Proud
- Arrogant
- Expects to be served
- Never serves
- Demands respect

Appearance

- Handsome
- Beautiful
- Neat
- Smart
- Careful
- Smile
- Pleasant
- Good shape
- Active
- Careless
- Unkempt
- Dirty
- Rough
- Fat
- Skinny

CHECKPOINT

Physical Appearance	Profession	Spiritual	Character

How did you do? Did you select any bad items for the person you want to marry? I guess you picked the most admirable and loving qualities. If you picked any negative item for your spouse, why did you do that? If you did not choose any negative item, why is that?

COMPLETE YOUR LOVE BOX

Now you will be presented with two boxes below, you are going to select some attributes from both boxes to create a third box. But this time, there are limitations as to what you can choose. You are creating your own box but from both boxes.

Box 1		
Caring	Prayerful	Faithful
Generous	Humble	Forgiving
Patience	Intelligent	Tall
Funny	Rich	Educated
Friendly	Pretty	Romantic
Handsome	Beautiful	Matured
Respectful	Kind	Smart

Box 2		
Rude	Arrogant	Selfish
Unforgiving	Lazy	Sexy
Unbeliever	Impatient	Rich
Strong	Handsome	Beautiful
Liar	Unfaithful	Mean
Stingy	Bully	Poor
Unkempt	Careless	Disrespectful

Box 3

Select 10 from Box 1, and 10 from Box 2.

You can see that Box 1 contains pleasant attributes, and Box 2 contains Not So *pleasant attributes.*

WHAT DOES THIS EXERCISE MEAN?

You can create an ideal person in your head, and that is what we all do especially when you are younger.

You create your Prince Charming or a beautiful princess, who is flawless, hoping to meet them very soon, and live happily ever after! But we know this hardly happens. Many people have high hopes and standards in their younger age and as they mature, they become more realistic and revise their wish list.

Hence Box 3, which means you now must be more accommodating. You accept certain flaws of your potential spouse as you realise that you also have some flaws, and someone will have to put up with you.

Let's look at what influences many people's choices, apart from desire. Why do they choose person A over person B, even if they do not know themselves well?

> *"But if you are vigilant, many behaviours will also be seen, either at the beginning, or in the middle of the relationship."*

CHAPTER 12

The Right Woman to Marry

"And the Lord God said, It is not good
that the man should be alone;
I will make him a help meet for him."

GENESIS 2:18 KJV

"Eagles do not compete with chickens.
Virtuous ladies know their price and grace
they carry. They rise above worldly patterns
to create a beautiful and godly family."

Most of you have desires in your heart for qualities and characters you are expecting from ladies you want to marry. But not all young men know this because they are either not yet ready or not sure what to look for in a woman to marry. Some of you desire a woman with physical attributes such as height, shape, legs and even the way they talk. Every one of you has inbuilt attractions that only you know. **But I would also want you to consider the following enduring and stable qualities in the woman you want to marry.**

SEVEN POWERFUL QUALITIES OF A POTENTIAL MRS RIGHT

1. Marry a Helpful Woman

> *"And the Lord God said, It is not good that the man should be alone; I will make him an help meet for him."*
>
> GENESIS 2:18 KJV

'Helpmeet' (KJV) in the original

Hebrew *'ezer kanegdo' is used –*

Ezer simply means: *A helper, supporter, or someone who provides aid or succour.* Interestingly, this word is often used in the Bible to describe God as a helper to humanity.

Kanegdo means: *"corresponding to him"*, or *"a counterpart for him."* This word implies equality and partnership, emphasizing that the woman is to complement and complete the man.

Oxford Dictionary describes 'succour' as the following:

"Help that you give to somebody who is suffering or having problems. Example: To give/bring succour to the sick and wounded."

So, you can see how important it is to choose a wife who is kind and compassionate. One who will come speedily with your help. One who will not tarry when you call. They are like your roadside insurance for your car, AA or Green flag! They are also like the ambulance!

She should not only help you with her intelligence and emotional support. She must be willing to support with her money and properties and all she has.

'Ezer' woman is likened to a Saviour. A typical *'ezer'* woman is compared to Psalm 121.

> *"I will lift up mine eyes unto the hills,*
> *from whence cometh my help. My help cometh*
> *from the Lord, which made heaven and earth."*
>
> PSALM 121:1-2

'Help' here is also *'ezer,'* which means succour. This help comes from the Lord. It means that if you find a woman who is a helper, you have found someone with the nature of God.

If you found a woman who is ready to ignore all the equality noises and collaborate with you with all her gifts, you have an 'ezer' woman.

2. Marry a Suitable Woman – 'Ezer Kanegdo'

God did not give Adam a perfect wife! What did he give him? **A suitable wife!** What does this mean? Eve might not be the most beautiful woman, holy and obedient, but she was suitable for Adam.

Depending on your nature, temperament, background and training, God can help you find a wife who will be able to cope with most of your strengths and weaknesses. A woman who is just right for you! A woman who will appreciate you the way you are. Remember you are not an angel. You have your own faults, so don't expect to have a faultless wife.

Evans is a young minister of God who married Diana three years ago. Evans says, "When I met Di, I was surprised that no one was dating her. But I also counted myself lucky. She complements me in every way. I love cooking, but Di is not quite keen. I love driving, she hates it. She loves washing up and cleaning, these chores, I detest them. My mother was always worried about me for not wanting to do those chores but look at what God has done. He has given me not just a beautiful wife but the one who covers my weaknesses and flaws. She supports my ministry with all her gifts. She is so suitable and perfect for me. I cannot believe I got so lucky!"

You can see that if you are not Diana, it may be very hard to marry Evans. His training and background are different. If Evans just wanted any girl to marry, they would have a lot of difficulties. Because Evans hates cleaning, that would put many ladies off. But Di finds cleaning therapeutic. The time to be alone with herself! She is thankful to God for marrying Evans.

So, somebody's wife cannot be your wife! And somebody's husband cannot also be your husband. ***If you are a king, ask God to help you marry a lady who is prepared to be a princess or a queen. If you have an ambition to be a minister, ask God to help you find a woman who will be happy to be a minister's wife!***

3. Marry Favour

> *"He who finds a wife finds a good thing,*
> *and obtains favour from the Lord."*
>
> PROVERBS 18:22 NKJV

If you find the *'ezer'* woman, you have found favour. Blessings and favour will follow you wherever you go. Singles and young men should do whatever it takes to find this woman full of favour. A woman who is God-fearing. **This woman will transform your world, your life and your fortunes.**

4. Marry a Woman With Unfading Beauty of Gentle and Quiet Spirit

This is another blockbuster and beautiful virtue! This cannot be picked from any shop floor. You either have it or you don't.

This virtuous woman will just bring her case to God in prayer instead of quarrelling with her husband. They are usually prayerful and prophetesses. They may possess a great deal of wisdom even though they may not speak much. It is difficult to spot them from afar. You must get very close to them to appreciate their beauty which is derived from within.

The smiles and words of such women leave a lasting imprint in your life. They dress modestly and do not call attention to themselves. **Women of gentle and quiet spirit are so considerate and kind in all things. They are a gem! Most men without discernment will pass them by without noticing their presence. But if God shines your eye to meet this woman, you have found a perfect wife!**

Phyllis and I have been married for 25 years. I can tell you that some people still ask me how I got so lucky. For me, it is not about just her physical attraction, it is the gentle spirit, wisdom and grace that she carries. These qualities have been a blessing to me and the family. Men ought to open their eyes to such inner qualities that last a long time!

5. Marry a Virtuous Woman

> *"Who can find a virtuous woman?*
> *for her price is far above rubies."*
>
> PROVERBS 31:10 KJV

The Hebrew word, '*chayil*' is translated as virtuous. It is such a powerful word that embodies the totality of an amazing woman to marry.

It means the following:

- Wealth
- Force of an army
- Strength

- Ability
- Efficiency
- God-fearing
- Nobility

If you are lucky enough to meet her, you must grab her with both hands and feet! You have found not just a gem, in fact, you have found an ideal wife!

6. Marry a Woman Who Fears the Lord

> *"Charm is deceptive, and beauty is fleeting; but a woman who fears the Lord is to be praised."*
>
> PROVERBS 31:30 NIV

Physical attributes and beauty are not just desirable they are also quite charming. Most men are on the lookout for a beautiful woman to marry. Of course, the woman you marry must be attractive to you physically, but you must define beauty in your own sight. Listen to the king of romance, King Solomon, who says that the woman who fears the Lord shall be praised.

You see, it is not the beautiful woman who will be praised. A woman who puts her trust and hope in the Lord. A woman who does what the Bible recommends. A woman who will support your ministry. A woman who will stand with you in prayer. A woman who loves the word of God! A woman who will help you train your children in the Lord! A woman who will submit to the authority of God, not what the world says! **This woman is worthy of your attention!**

7. Marry an Intelligent Woman

> *"His name was Nabal and his wife's name was Abigail. She was an intelligent and beautiful woman, but her husband was surly and mean in his dealings—he was a Calebite."*
>
> 1 SAMUEL 25:3 NIV

The intelligence of Abigail was supreme! Her humility that shone through her personality was unbelievable! Fast thinker! Forward-looking! Saviour of the family!

Intelligent women like Abigail will save you and your family when you have been silly. Intelligent women will see the danger first and help you take cover. An intelligent woman will be your advisor, counsellor, and your defender. She will not nag you and send you to the rooftop, nor send you wandering in the desert!

> *"Better to live in a desert than with a quarrelsome and nagging wife."*
>
> PROVERBS 21:19 NIV

A wise woman has a way of speaking to your heart. She would not like to put you down when you make mistakes. She understands that as you try to support and protect the family, you will make mistakes, but she is prepared to forgive you. She is prepared to encourage you and lift you up. **In fact, she is so skilled in winning not just your heart, she makes you feel like a champion and a king!**

WHERE TO FIND MY 'EZER' WOMAN

You may not spot them in nightclubs or at the discos. In fact, you may not see them loitering on the street. Their appearances may not be full of makeup. They may not wear brands or designers. They may not talk much to draw your attention. They may not be one of those girls who throw themselves at you for your compliments.

Find Them Buried

They are a rare gem. **They are not on the surface of the soil. They are buried deep in the soil. To find them, you must dig very deep.** It requires a lot of effort and diligence. It requires prayer and fasting. It requires a lot of discerning to separate them from the other girls. ***May you find your 'ezer' woman as you begin your search in Jesus' name.***

Find Her in God's House

As a believer, your first place of search is in the house of God. **This woman of God is constantly in the presence of God, seeking a kind man with a gentle heart to offer their amazing skills, talents and power to support him.** If you are also in the presence of God all the time, you should not miss her.

You probably sit next to her in every church service or stand together and pray. Maybe you have not bothered to even ask her name. You probably meet her at conventions. You may also meet her at your university campus, PENSA or Christian meetings. Maybe she is your friend who prays with you. I can hear someone saying it is not possible to marry girls you grew up with in the church. I say it is best to marry your friend if they are attracted to you.

CHECKPOINT

List five core things that you want to find in the woman you want to marry:

"This woman of God is constantly in the presence of God, seeking a kind man with a gentle heart to offer their amazing skills, talents and power to support him."

CHAPTER 13

The Right Man to Marry

"Husbands, in the same way be considerate as you live with your wives, and treat them with respect as the weaker partner and as heirs with you of the gracious gift of life, so that nothing will hinder your prayers."

1 PETER 3:7 NIV

"Don't be fooled by the beauty and glamour of wedding ceremonies and the wedding gowns; marriage can be extremely stressful and hard work, especially for a woman."

The desire for equality and freedom from oppressive husbands over the years, has changed how women select their potential husbands. Gone are the days when women were given or sold as commodities to men, especially rich men. Leah was given to Jacob without her consent. Many women suffered the same fate. We thank God this has changed.

Women now have the right to choose the man who will be their husbands, and rightly so. Equality also means women will still have to carry babies for nine months, and men will carry that equally, but women will still have to go through menstrual cycles alone, sometimes with pain. They will still have to be homemakers. They will still have to go to work the same hours as men. They will earn the same money as men.

It has changed from when men were the breadwinners, to men and women now being breadwinners. If you are fortunate to have a supporting husband, they will help you with chores, and the children. That is why it is your responsibility to select a man who will not leave everything to you. It is way too much.

If the stakes in marriage are high for young men, it is even higher for the ladies. The biological clock means you need a stable relationship, or marriage within a certain time frame. This puts pressure on single women to marry as soon as possible. **Divorce hurts the woman more than the man. It is therefore critical that you do not rush into marriage just because your biological clock is ticking!**

Men find substitutes for their wives quite easily. Separation can be too stressful for ladies who are known to be wired emotionally to their husbands. This means that if the boys want a good wife, the girls should demand great husbands. But ladies, if you are careful, there are many men with great potential out there. Pray and select only one whom you can love and submit to.

> ***"Pray and select only one whom you can love and submit to."***

EIGHT DESIRABLE QUALITIES OF A POTENTIAL MR RIGHT

1. Marry a Man and a Champion

> *"Therefore, shall a man leave his father and his mother, and shall cleave unto his wife: and they shall be one flesh."*
>
> GENESIS 2:24 KJV

Ladies, the ball is now on your court. Now that you are in your prime, take your time before you say 'yes'. Do not marry a big baby boy. Do not marry a child. It is a criminal offence to do that. ***In the scripture above, it says "a man leaves". Babies don't leave their parents.*** You have a duty and responsibility to marry a male who is also grown and mature.

The Hebrew word for 'man' is '*iysh*' (pronounced 'eesh') which also means the following:

- **Husband** – The person should have already become a husband material.
- **Servant** – The man is ready to serve you and your children. In fact, he is already serving in his church, family and community. He is down to earth. Not arrogant.
- **Mankind** – He is a human being with a human heart. He is a kind man.
- **Champion** – He is a champion undefeated by situations and circumstances. He never gives up easily. He will fight for you and to save you.
- **Great man** – He is a mighty man. He is a noble and honourable man. He is full of wisdom. He is intelligent. He is well respected.

"You have a duty and responsibility to marry a male who is also grown and mature."

2. Marry a Man of God

Here, I am not referring to people who parade themselves with titles, but no substance. They call themselves MoG but are sleeping around with girls. Also, not those who go to church but cannot even give you 10 scriptures to save you if you were kidnapped. I am talking about a man who is in the presence of God. Just like Adam in the Garden of Eden. Eden means pleasure. It also represents the presence of God.

> *"The Lord God took the man and put him in the Garden of Eden to work it and take care of it."*
>
> GENESIS 2:15 NIV

Your man must NOT only be found in the presence of God. He must be seen to be delighted in the presence of God. He must be fully committed to God. He is serving the Lord and the congregation. He is truly a man of God living pure and holy life as he waits for you to join him. He is not a man who wants you to prove you love him by having sex with him! He does not only respect you, but he has full respect for God and his word!

"He must be seen to be delighted in the presence of God."

3. Marry a Man Who is Working

> *"God put Adam in the Garden of Eden to work in it and to take care of it."*
>
> GENESIS 2:15 NIV

The man you must marry is one who is working. He has a job that brings home money. It does not matter how much money you earn; your man must be in employment, or a vocation that earns money. Marriage requires money. When your man tells you he is a man of God and God will provide, please think again. No excuses. If they are not working, they are not ready to marry.

Cyndi, 40, said, "When I met my husband, Paul, he assured me that he was not working but as a faithful man, he believed God would look after us. I was working as an account clerk. My take-home pay was not much. It became worse when I had 2 children in the first two years of marriage. When I was on maternity leave, it was too hard, I had to return to work quickly. After 4 years of pain and no financial support, I quit the marriage. I was broken. I was tired and worn out. I looked like an old woman at 30 years. My advice is that if a man is not working, be careful to marry him."

4. Marry a Man Who Will Leave to Cleave

If he has not already left his father and mother, he must be ready to leave as soon as possible. What does leaving mean?

The Hebrew word for 'leave' is '*awzab*', which means the following:

- To loosen
- Forsake
- Depart from
- Leave behind
- Let alone
- Abandon
- Neglect
- Apostatise (abandonment or renunciation).

These are strong words. They are not words for children. They seem harsh and inconsiderate on their parents, but I'm afraid that is exactly what it is. You either leave or you don't.

In the words of Theresa May (Former British Prime Minister), *"leave means leave"*. When we leave our job, we pack all our decorations in the office, personal files and certificates, we say goodbye and walk out. Sometimes, there is a little party at the office to mark your leaving and the start of your new adventure. In the UK, if you are a senior or a big boss, not only do you walk out, but your access to the company IT system, your emails, door or gate pass are quickly deactivated. All staff are required to leave behind their company uniforms, and even car park pass.

You are leaving, that is it. You do not report to your boss anymore and you only come back there when invited. **This time, someone else must let you in. You do not have any more privileges in this company. You have left.**

> *"Therefore, shall a man leave his father*
> *and his mother, and shall cleave unto his wife:*
> *and they shall be one flesh."*
>
> GENESIS 2:24 KJV

If that man gives you excuses, such as, "I cannot leave now," "Me and my parents are close," or "We need to find accommodation close to them," etcetera, think twice before you say 'yes' to him.

Leaving can be both physical space and emotional attachment. Sometimes it is right to leave the physical space or environment to prove that you are a man. You might also have to break the parental emotional stranglehold by refusing to call them all the time or pick up their regular calls. This is how we leave them!

However, you still belong to a family as per culture. You still have a duty of care towards your parents especially when they are old. Break away from their control when you marry but be a responsible son. Listen to what the wise man said ...

> *"Listen to your father, who gave you life, and do not despise your mother when she is old."*
>
> PROVERBS 23:22 NIV

Learn to be a man who is attached to his wife but detached from the control of the father and mother. It is a balancing act you must do with wisdom and consideration,

"Leaving can be both physical space and emotional attachment."

5. Marry the Sensible Ones, Avoid the Nabals

Nabal was a wealthy man who benefited from family fortunes and inheritance. Sadly, the Bible describes him as a fool. He was a rich fool. In fact, his name Nabal coincidentally means, 'a fool'. Maybe due to his wealth, he was lucky to marry one of the most intelligent and beautiful women on earth, Abigail. She said this to King David,

> *"Please pay no attention, my lord, to that wicked man Nabal. He is just like his name—his name means Fool, and folly goes with him. And as for me, your servant, I did not see the men my lord sent."*
>
> 1 SAMUEL 25:25 NIV

If you are an Abigail, beautiful and intelligent woman, you deserve a godly king to marry. Do not rush to marry a Nabal. There are Josephs, Daniels and Davids. Do not let a man's money, car or possessions alone become your target. **Have discerning eyes and spirit to sift the Davids from the Nabals.**

6. Marry a Man Who Knows the True Meaning of Love

Some men are amazing when it comes to love. They epitomise 1 Corinthians 13. When you see them, in fact, you see 'love'. They are patient, kind, gentle, compassionate, forgiving, trustworthy and protective. Not only that, but they also give themselves to make their spouses pure and holy. They also love you just like they love their bodies. This man, you can refer to as Mr Love.

On the contrary, some men are selfish, greedy, mean, unforgiving, arrogant and difficult to live with. They have no concept of love. It is all about them and themselves. Beware of such men even if they have all possessions.

Chantel, 35, married for six years to Joe says, "I dreaded getting married. My parents' marriage scared me off. That is why I did not get married until I was 29 years old. Joe has proved to me there are still genuine men out there who can be trusted. He is the embodiment of love itself. I feel appreciated. I feel safe. I feel loved. He is prayerful, honest, considerate and so respectful. Marrying him is the best decision I have ever made in my life!"

7. Marry a Respectful Man

You need a man who will not only respect you but your parents and your family. A man who respects you as a partner, and not as a servant. Women preparing to marry should open their eyes beyond physicality and read clearly what is in the heart and soul of the man to be their husband.

Young ladies, ideal men for you should respect your opinions and respect you as the most important person on earth, even above any woman. He should value your presence and your absence. He should respect your marriage bed and should cherish your body and relationship.

"Husbands, in the same way, be considerate as you live with your wives, and treat them with respect as the weaker partner and as heirs with you of the gracious gift of life, so that nothing will hinder your prayers."

1 PETER 3:7 NIV

"He should value your presence and your absence"

8. Marry a Man Who is Considerate

Considerate means you care about and respect them and their space and opinion. It also means you are careful not to inconvenience or harm others.

"Husbands, in the same way be considerate as you live with your wives, and treat them with respect as the weaker partner and as heirs with you of the gracious gift of life, so that nothing will hinder your prayers."

1 PETER 3:7

They say size matters! Because men are generally bulky and taller, they feel powerful over women. It is great to have great physique, but it should not be used to intimidate your wife. **It should rather be used to make her feel safe and secure in your presence!**

Marriage can be fun and exciting especially if your man, who is your leader, is kind and considerate towards you and others. Sad to say that some men use their size to harm their wives and children. A man who is considerate is a beautiful man! A considerate man is a peaceful man! When you are dating, please look out for this man. How are they considerate towards another person?

A considerate man feels for your suffering and pain. A considerate man is empathetic!

When he is driving, does he have road rage and call people names, insulting them? If they are respectful and considerate towards their family members, sisters and the public, they will be towards you. If they are not, the chance that they would be considerate towards you is very small.

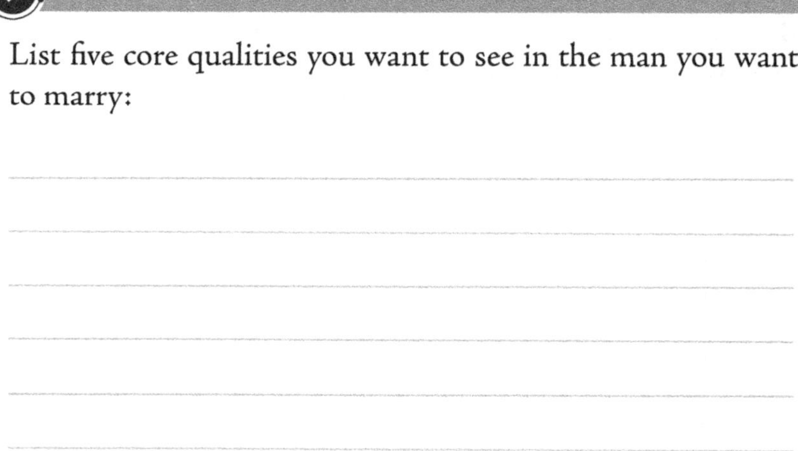

List five core qualities you want to see in the man you want to marry:

"A considerate man is sympathetic to your suffering hurt. A considerate man is compassionate towards you. A considerate man feels for your suffering and pain. A considerate man is empathetic!"

SECTION FOUR

LOVE BEYOND FEELINGS AND SEX

CHAPTER 14

Love and Sex

"And now these three remain: faith, hope and love. But the greatest of these is love."

1 CORINTHIANS 13:13 NIV

"Faith makes all things possible... love makes all things easy."

DWIGHT L. MOODY

Love has always been a topic of great interest because everyone wants to be loved. Most people will also seek love in a relationship at some point in their lives. Especially when you are young, all you dream about is growing up quickly so you can fall in love with a boy or a girl. *Due to pressure and influence from the community and social media, the meaning and understanding of love is shifting towards one area, Sex!*

Lucy ran home one winter evening with a great smile on her face. "Parents, I have breaking news! My boyfriend Matt has proposed to me." She pulled her hand from her pocket and showed them her ring finger, glistening with an engagement ring. Dad looked down with discomfort as if he was disinterested but kept quiet. Her mother, a typical Nigerian mother looked at her also bemused and asked, "What does this mean Lucy?" Lucy replied with energy, "Mom, we love each other, and we are going to marry by the end of next year." Dad jumped in, "What do you 19-year-old girl know and understand of love?" Lucy says, "Dad, Matt is 22 years old, he is old enough to understand love! I am in love with him, and I cannot live without marrying him."

When young people say they are in love, many parents dread this because they are not sure what kind of love their children are talking about. Unfortunately, they do not have conversations with the young people about what they mean. This is because many adults who thought they were in love in their youthful ages ended up divorcing. They realised quickly after one or two bouts of sexual intercourse that the feeling of love had disappeared! To them, love was all a façade! It was not as deep as they thought. It was just a temporary, transient feeling compelled by their hormones! It was more infatuation than love! Their so-called love experience left them with a sour taste in their mouth!

They are now very protective in ensuring that their children do not fall into the same trap. But I guess everybody's experience about love is different.

I did not enter a full relationship until I was 27 years old. Even then, I experienced many lows in love but my overall experience with love has been amazing. I am not afraid for my children to enter relationships when they are mature. I married at the age of 32. I do not expect them to wait that long but there are great benefits to understanding love before you enter a relationship.

Lucy did not tell her family she was sleeping with Matt. She is only going out with him. But in the parents' mind, Lucy is probably sleeping with Matt once they say they are in love. It is what young people do when they go out. Her parents are stressing. Besides when young people have sex, they say they are in love!

It may be casual sex, a one-night stand or fornicating, they prefer to call it lovemaking! *You must open your eyes widely, so that you do not fall for the bait of love. It is also important that you do not sell your love or chase love!*

It is important to define love in its purest and godliest form. For those who belong to the Christian faith, it is important to understand the original context and intention of love. **To think that love is equated to sex is normal in this current dispensation, but it is a false start to a relationship!** In fact, many youths are selling or buying love as though it is a market commodity. Rushing into love, or into a relationship, is like a person who has not passed his driving test and yet bent on driving a car at all costs.

> ***"Rushing into love, or into a relationship, is like a person who has not passed his driving test and yet bent on driving a car at all costs."***

WHAT PEOPLE SAY ABOUT LOVE

- Andy, 29, and married for one year says, *"For me, you do not love me if you do not prioritise me above all others – priority."*
- Amanda, 24, and single says, *"Loving me is not easy but you must be close to me and spend time with me."*
- Erica, 52, says, *"My love has changed over the years. But one thing stands out, I need to feel your presence, your skin and feel validated by you."*

- Amy, 23, single says, *"If a guy says he loves me, he must be patient with me, generous to me and ready to give me hugs."*
- Dan, 36, married for 4 years says, *"If a woman loves me, I expect her to respect me, be happy to see me and open up to me."*
- Frank, 32, says, *"We need to hang out, and spend quality time together. Love me and love who I am."*
- Josephine, 28, and married says, *"Love to me is not all about sex, I know. But you cannot love me if you don't want to sleep with me when we are married. I need cuddles, kisses and sex. But the biggest need for me is communicating with me and showing me affection."*
- Grace, 50, and married for 24 years says, *"When we were younger, flowers, going out and hanging out was love to me. But now spending time with me, showing kindness and empathy to me is all that matters to me in love."*

THE DICTIONARY DEFINITION OF LOVE IS CONFUSING

Both the Cambridge and Oxford dictionaries have about 24 definitions each for love. One that attracts me from the Cambridge dictionary is:

"To like another adult very much and be romantically and sexually attracted to them, or to have strong feelings of liking a friend or person in your family."

Three things that stand out here are:

- To like an adult very much
- Romantic attraction
- Strong feelings

There are so many emotions and feelings that resemble love, so you must continue to read the following topics to appreciate people's intentions. Feelings can be influenced by simple things like weather of the day, smell of perfume, hormones and many others.

WHAT DOES THE BIBLE SAY?

The Bible also does not define 'love' by using one word. It defines 'love' through the demonstration of actions. It defines 'love' by what you do or show towards your fellow human beings. Does the Bible make it easy for you? Probably not. Especially if you are not sure that the person's love towards you is romantic (*eros*) or brotherly love (*philadelphia*).

Love is a demonstration of action. But God demonstrates his own love for us in this:

> *"While we were still sinners, Christ died for us."*
>
> ROMANS 5:8 NIV

Here, love is seen through the demonstration of action. That action is dying for someone you love! Will you die for the one you claim you love? Paul defines love as patient and kind:

> *"Love is patient, love is kind. It does not envy,*
> *it does not boast, it is not proud."*
>
> 1 CORINTHIANS 13:4 NIV

Here the Bible's definition of love is being patient and kind to someone. If someone is patient and kind to me, is he or she in love with me?

THE SUPREMACY OF LOVE

"Three things will last forever, —faith, hope, and love—and the greatest of these is love."

1 CORINTHIANS 13:13 NLT

Faith, hope and love are three powerful virtues that will endure or continue forever. But love is the greatest of them! We will explore further why love is supreme.

"Without love, faith is nothing but empty religious gymnastics!"

FIVE REASONS WHY LOVE IS *THE ULTIMATE, THE KING AND SUPREME VIRTUE*

1. Both Faith and Hope Depend on Love for Their Existence

Faith does not exist without love. **Without love, faith is nothing but empty religious gymnastics!**

"If I have a faith that can move mountains, but do not have love, I am nothing."

1 CORINTHIANS 13:2 NIV

Faith and hope come alive in the presence of love. If you perform all miracles and have faith that can move mountains but have no love, your faith is in vain. That means, your hope and faith are valid demonstrations of your love. In fact, this is true in every type of love. Whether you love them brotherly or romantically, you must demonstrate with action. If your brother is hungry and you have food, you should not be praying for them to get food. You cannot hope they get fed if you are praying in faith for them whilst you have food stored elsewhere. You should feed them rather.

2. Love is the Essential Nature of God

Love is the embodiment of God. Love comes from God. In fact, God is love!

> *"Whoever does not love does not know God,*
> *because God is love."*
>
> 1 JOHN 4:8 NIV

This is deeper than you think. Many of you think you love God. But you hate your brother. You hate your spouse. Hate does not come from God. Love comes from God. All Christians must have love because their Father's DNA contains love that He passes onto those who get born again.

3. Love Serves Others

Hope and faith benefit the user.

> *"A new command I give you: Love one another.*
> *As I have loved you, so you must love one another.*
> *By this everyone will know that you are*
> *my disciples, if you love one another."*
>
> JOHN 13:34-35 NIV

It is your Christian responsibility to love others, especially those who are Christians. Supporting them where they are weak, and you are strong. For instance, we do not go to church just to pray, sing hymns and come home. It is a fellowship. Fellow men in the same ship. Fellow women in the same ship. You must be on the lookout for those who will benefit from your service and help them.

Anyone who gives to the poor, lends it to the Lord. This means that, when you are in need, the Lord will also remember you! **Hope and faith edify yourself, but Love benefits other people.**

In love we give out! It is more blessing to give than to receive! In love we serve others and God. But hope and faith edify us.

> ***"Hope and faith edify ourselves,***
> ***but in love we serve others and God."***

4. Love is Spirit

> *"And hope does not put us to shame, because God's love has been poured out into our hearts through the Holy Spirit, who has been given to us."*
>
> ROMANS 5:5 NIV

We have already learnt that hope lives because of love. But importantly, love is poured in our hearts by the Holy Spirit, who is also God. It is why as a Christian you should not struggle to love if you are born again. The spirit of Love coming from the Holy Spirit dwells in your heart.

If you are in a relationship, it is your duty to ensure that whatever your reason for going into marriage, the love comes from the Holy Spirit. Your feeling must not be lust, selfish gain, or ambition. Simply put, you must be led by the Holy Spirit in love!

5. Love is the Greatest Commandment

There are several commandments out there including theTen Commandments. The scholars asked Jesus which of them was the greatest. Jesus did not say hope, faith or miracles.

> *"Jesus replied: 'Love the Lord your God with all your heart and with all your soul and with all your mind.' This is the first and greatest commandment. And the second is like it: 'Love your neighbour as yourself.'"*
>
> MATTHEW 22:37-39 NIV

There are two greatest commandments – love your neighbour and love your God! If you can do these two, you have fulfilled all the law! You can see that love is deeper than what the world and the internet makes us believe. When you say you love someone, you are touching the very heart of God. It is a sweet aroma, that is pleasing to him.

6. Love Never Fails

"Love lasts forever because God lasts forever."

Another key reason love is supreme is its longevity! Hope and faith may fail. They may disappoint but true love stays the same. Whether rain or shine, through mountains and valleys! Through the pressures and troubles of this world, love should remain. It should be unmoved, and it should be unshakable! **Loving someone means you have dedicated all your life to them. It should not fall apart. It should hold on till eternity.**

You can see from the ongoing discussion that the root of love is very deep. It is difficult to uproot! It is too strong to fail. It is the very nature of God. He is present in your heart and in your love. He will help anyone who loves correctly to succeed for his own name's sake.

When you decide you love someone you should weigh them against the characteristics above. Will your anchor of love hold in the storms of love? If your anchor holds, your love is of God!

CHECKPOINT

What is the meaning of love to you?

How do you expect your boyfriend or girlfriend to show they love you? List three things:

"When you say you love someone, you are touching the very heart of God."

CHAPTER 15

Flavours of Love

"To love someone is nothing,
to be loved by someone is something,
to love someone who loves you is everything."

BILL RUSSELL

WHY WE LOVE

Falling in love can be easy but falling out of love is painful and heartbreaking. It can be very expensive and costly. You need to know why someone says they love you. It is important to know if they love you because of what you possess or what they can get from you. In this section you will explore the meaning of true love and other flavours of love.

When I was younger, I had to fight for the attention of my single mother. Six siblings, one mother! It was always the one who shouted the loudest that got the attention of my poor mother. When I did something right, I got praised and rewarded by her. When I made mistakes, what came next was the rod! I grew up with the understanding that you earn love by doing something right. My perception was that love was not free; it was something you worked to earn!

To people who come from a rejected or deprived family background like me, love means acceptance. If you accept them the way they are, they feel you love them. To the hungry, providing food for them is a sure sign of your love. To the poor, to love them may mean meeting their needs or giving them money. To the illegal immigrant, if you can marry them so they can obtain the right documentation to live in the country, you have shown incredible love to them.

Love means different things to different people. Let's dissect the types of love out there.

TYPES OF LOVE

This contemporary world and the internet have come up with several types of love. But the Greek word for love can mean several things, such as:

- '*Ludus*': flirtatious, playful, casual, uncommitted.
- '*Pragma*': committed, long-standing.
- '*Philautia*': self-love.
- '*Mania*': obsessive, possessive, addictive, dependent.
- '*Philia*': friendship love.
- '*Storge*': family love.
- '*Eros*': romantic love.
- '*Agape*': God kind of love.

However, the four main components of love found in the New Testament are: '*philia*', '*storge*', '*eros*' *and* '*agape*'.

> ***"Love means different things to different people."***

'PHILIA' LOVE – FRIENDSHIP

This is generally called brotherly or friendship love. It is a deep affectionate and loyal friendship expressed between people who share similar interests. The Bible talks a lot about brotherly love, or '*Philadelphia*'! There are close bonds that exist between the people involved but they are not sexual or romantic.

An example is found in Hebrews:

> *"Let brotherly love continue."*
>
> HEBREWS 13:1 KJV

In '*philia*' love, friendship means: ***Companionship, Communication, Cooperation and Compassion.*** This kind of love can easily be misinterpreted as romantic love if friends in the church do not define the nature of their love early.

Hilda broke down when Ken, her best friend in church, revealed to her that he had started going out with another girl. "We sing in the choir together. We have been playing together since I was 15 and he was 16. At my 21st birthday, a few guys showed interest in me, but I rejected them. I thought that Ken loved me."

Ken says, "I never showed any romantic interest or talked about love with Hilda. We have been friends. I love her as a sister. She knows everything about me. How can we get married? There is nothing more than brotherly love."

Young singles should be careful not to read too much meaning into every kindness and relationship, as if it is romantic love leading to marriage. *It is better to define your relationship with the opposite sex earlier on in your friendship. Some of the friendships can ultimately develop, grow and lead to a romantic relationship with time. But this should not be rushed or assumed.*

'STORGE' LOVE (STORE-GAY)

This is the love you feel for your family members. It is also the love that parents have for their children. There is a natural connection to our family regardless of whether they love us back or not.

> *"Be devoted to one another in love.*
> *Honor one another above yourselves."*
>
> ROMANS 12:10 NIV

Love here is the Greek word *'philostorgos'* which is translated as mutual love of parents and children and wives and husbands.

Peter said "My brother Eric is a waste of space. Anything including money I give to him, he wastes it. It is hard for me because he is my brother. I cannot stand to see him struggling, so I keep helping. I hope and pray he changes because I still love him as a brother."

Usually, when a member of your family is in trouble, you go to every extent to help them out. Read the account below reported by BBC in April 2022:

Within days of Russia's invasion, Anastasia Pavlova understood what the war was going to mean for Ukraine. The 23-year-old escaped the bombardment of Kharkiv, a city where shelling of residential areas was "indiscriminate" – in the words of the local mayor – from the start. Anastasia and her fiancé Abakelia went south to the city of Dnipro. She felt safer here in the tower block apartment of Abakelia's family. But she agonised over the fate of her own parents, who lived on the outskirts of Mariupol. They risked everything and drove back to bring her parents to safety. They could have died themselves.

This is how strong *'storge'* love can be. It is forceful and demanding. It reminds you of all the great times you have shared with your parents, brothers and sisters. Love will make a demand for you to do whatever you can to help them. You feel very responsible for them.

It is *'storge'* love in action! It is incest to romantically love your family members. You cannot miss this!

> ***"Love will make a demand for you to do whatever you can to help them."***

'EROS' LOVE

This is the Greek word for physical, romantic, or sexual love. In Greek mythology, Eros is the god of love, desire, lust and sex. *'Eros'* is the root of the word erotic, which means 'to arouse sexual desire or excitement'.

Eros usually makes demands on your groins and genitals. It can be full of fantasies and infatuations. It has the power to activate your flesh, the hormones and your instincts.

It is called erotic because it easily arouses your desires for sexual gratification and relationships. *'Eros'* love acts on your senses! The lust of the eyes, lust of the flesh, and pride of life! In the Bible, physical love will usually be used in the context of marriage.

But understand that *'eros'* is also important in your romantic relationship, especially in the early stages of falling in love. This is what brings that attraction and lust for the individual. In a sexually fulfilling marriage, a husband and wife will be physically attracted to one another romantically. Without this erotic attraction, many couples drift away to find love.

Peter, married for three years complained. "When we got married, I was all over Patricia in the first year. I found her so attractive and irresistible. I always wanted to kiss her and have sex with her. But since Junior was born a year ago, it has changed everything. The feeling has disappeared."

Married couples have a responsibility to keep the *'eros'* love going for as long as they can. This will protect the sanctity of their marriage.

'AGAPE' LOVE (AG-AH –PAY)

> *"But God demonstrates his own love for us in this: While we were still sinners, Christ died for us."*
>
> ROMAN 5:8 NIV

Totally committed love. It is Christ-like kind of love. Sacrificial, unconditional, forgiving and eternal. It is a selfless and giving love. It is love at its best! It is the benchmark to measure all true love!

This is the type of love defined by Apostle Paul in 1 Corinthians 13.

> *"Love is patient and kind. Love is not jealous or boastful or proud or rude. It does not demand its own way. It is not irritable, and it keeps no record of being wronged. It does not rejoice about injustice but rejoices whenever the truth wins out. Love never gives up, never loses faith, is always hopeful, and endures through every circumstance."*
>
> 1 CORINTHIANS 13:4-7. NLT

'Agape' is a deep kind of love that can exist between brothers, parents, and all family members. It is the same kind of love that can exist between church members and community members.

For any real romantic relationship to thrive, you need *'agape'* love to be fully in action!

Seven characteristics of 'agape' love:

- It is kind
- Rejoices with the truth
- Always Protects
- Always Trusts
- Always hopes
- Always perseveres
- It is patient

If you are in a relationship or married, you can test yourself against the above standards if your love is genuine.

"'Agape' is a deep kind of love that can exist between brothers, parents, and all family members"

'AGAPE' LOVE COMES FROM GOD

> *"Dear friends, let us continue to love one another, for love comes from God. Anyone who loves is a child of God and knows God. But anyone who does not love does not know God, for God is love."*
>
> 1 JOHN 4:7-8 NLT

Agape is Perfect Love

There is no fear in love. But perfect love drives out fear, because fear has to do with punishment. The one who fears is not made perfect in love. (1 John 4:18 NIV)

A perfect relationship is not one devoid of argument or misunderstanding. Couples in a perfect relationship do not dread, they are not stricken by terror. Even when you have disagreements, you have no fears that they will do you any harm. It is the perfect love.

You are probably asking yourself if perfect love is achievable in this present age? Has anyone ever been perfect in their love and marriage? I was talking to a friend who said to me he has a perfect marriage. I asked him, *"Do you and your wife Angela have a perfect marriage?"* And he said, *"You can call it that way."* But I replied, *"Angels do not marry?"* I queried again.

He then quoted me this scripture in 1 John 4;18 to explain what he meant. Having deeply considered his argument, I am in favour of a perfect love and perfect marriage. **Your acid test for a perfect love therefore is not lack of disagreement or quarrel. It is the absence of FEAR in the relationship.**

The Greek word for fear is *'phobos'.* This means, 'dread, terror or that which strikes terror!' We are always afraid of God's judgment. But when we come to Christ, He loves us unconditionally, that judgment is taken away.

Couples should translate the same mind-set and concept into their relationships. Everyone fears criticism and judgment. Everyone dreads to meet persons who always put fear into them. **Couples in a perfect relationship do not dread, they are not stricken by terror.** They do not fear their partners will reject them. They do not fear they are hiding anything on their phones. They do not fear they will be dishonest. They do not fear they will misbehave when they are not together. They do not rejoice in their absence; they just feel their absence and wish they were with them. They have complete trust in them.

So, when you and your boyfriend or girlfriend who wants to marry you are together, ask yourself this question. *Is there anything I fear in this relationship? When I don't understand anything how open are they to clear my doubts and fears?* It is your duty to ensure that you have a perfect love for each other.

> ***"Couples in a perfect relationship do not dread, they are not stricken by terror."***

PLEASE LEARN WHAT LOVE IS NOT

When you are in romantic love, please don't close your eyes. In fact, make every effort not to be blinded by love. Love has the power to be intoxicating. Please resist that lure from love.

Romantic love has the attributes of 'agape' love, and more, and it is how I came to understand love. God through Paul has spelt out to us what love does not do. You must specialise in this first before you start jumping about being in love, after receiving a small gift and sweet talk.

The following can be part of falling in love, but on their own, they are not love. So, be wary of the following:

- **Envy** – When you are blessed with good things, they should be happy for you instead of being resentful.
- **Boasting** – They will not boast for their achievements, possessions or abilities to make you feel little or unworthy.
- **Pride** – They are full of themselves. When they love you, they are very considerate.
- **Dishonour** – They shame or disgrace you, especially in public. Love should rather honour you.

- **Self-seeking** – They have an interest in themselves alone. Love seeks your welfare and concern.
- **Easily angered** – They are mad at you for little mistakes. Love is not easily angered. They will be patient with you.
- **Keeping a record of wrongs** – Your mistakes are always referenced, kept in their head or written down.
- **Delight in evil** – When any misfortune happens to you, they are celebrating or accusing you, it is your fault.
- **Failing** – They will fail you at the slightest chance. Can they love you to the end?
- **Sweet talk** – They brag about what they don't even have.
- **Spiritual gifts** – Love is not a spiritual gift. Prophecy, healing, and faith having nothing to do with love.
- **Possessing all knowledge** – They are learned, academic and even have the gift of knowledge. That is not love.
- **Mountain moving faith** – They have great faith in removing mountains, healing the sick. But that is not love.
- **Understanding all God's mysteries** – They think they are so close to God; they understand all revelation and mystery. This one too, has nothing to do with love.
- **Ability to give to the poor** – In fact, they do not only give to the rich and family members. They also give to the poor. But check their motivations. Do not mistake this for love.

This is a summary from 1 Corinthians 13.

SEVEN TELLTALE SIGNS OF GENUINE LOVE

As a single person in a relationship or looking to fall in love with someone, you should look out for signs of love. They are not physical appearances. They are not fame and money. They are not qualifications. They are not prayer. They are not spiritual gifts, and they are not sex.

The signs are:

- **Kindness** – They are friendly, generous and considerate with you.
- **Patience** – It takes them so long before they are angry with you. They allow you time to finish what you need to do without complaining.
- **Truthful** – They rejoice when you have been truthful. They are also truthful. They will not lie to you.
- **Protection** – They are always protecting you physically and spiritually. They will defend you at all costs.
- **Trust** – They trust you and your judgment. They do not think they possess all the wisdom in the world.
- **Hope** – Even if things are not working well, they have confidence and hope it shall be well. They don't leave you and think you are done.
- **Persevere** – They are not giving up on you. They keep trying. They don't give up easily on any project. They are hardworking and very determined.

DON'T DO THIS

It is bad for you to also play with someone's heart by creating false hopes and expectations when you know very well that you do not love them. If you do not love them, avoid doing the following:

- Telling someone you love them
- Seducing someone
- Having sex with them
- Kissing them
- Spending unhindered time with them
- Having an emotional connection
- Showing affection
- Giving regular gifts
- Constant telephone conversation
- Proposing love or marriage
- Going out on a date
- Going on holiday together
- Going on 'bae-cation'
- Touching them intimately

When you do the above, you are creating false impressions that you are married. In fact, I do not recommend young people who are in a relationship to practice the above. It will give room to be tempted by the devil to sin.

There is a time and moment for everything. Wait until the appointed time for your marriage. Make your relationship perfect by being perfect yourself. Whatever you do not want others to do to you, do not do to others.

CHECKPOINT

List four things you fear if your relationship fails.

"Wait until the appointed time for your marriage. Make your relationship perfect by being perfect yourself."

CHAPTER 16

Beware of Fake Love!

This section is critical if you desire to find love. Here I will show you many fake loves. I will show you many reasons people fall into the wrong end of love. You will be able to check these against your feelings and the reality of love. I have already told you not everything is love. *Also, it takes great grace, prayer and vigilance to differentiate true love from fake love.*

This is because there are other emotions that present similar signs and symptoms as true love. Certain individuals with good personality ethics can deceive you into believing they love you. They will give you gifts of great value. They have learnt to say the right things to make you believe them. Some may present themselves as women or men of God. They will pray with you and even share the word of God with you. They will be persistent until they eventually steal your heart. They will speak into your beauty! They will appreciate your looks as none has ever done to you. They are all around you. They plot and scheme their tactics. They are eloquent and can even be generous. Please beware! Be careful not to quickly give them your heart before they pierce it with a sharp sword!

"Also, it takes great grace, prayer and vigilance to differentiate true love from fake love."

WHY DO PEOPLE BEHAVE THAT WAY?

It is difficult to know what is going through everyone's head. Not all beautiful and great-looking people you see on the street, at work and at church have great mental, psychological or spiritual well-being. Some people are aware of their mental and spiritual deficiencies whilst many others have no clue. It is possible you have some issues knowingly or unknowingly. Yet, you will still be attracted to someone. You will pursue or be pursued. When there is that feeling of love towards someone, you do not stop for once and think, am I correct? Am I actually alright to fall in love with this person? *Love is so controlling, that even the most disciplined individuals may fall for love!*

THIRTEEN REASONS THEY SAY THEY LOVE YOU

Let's investigate this in detail, the reasons why people are so quick to propose love, and why not every proposal is good or should be taken seriously.

1. Infatuation

This can wrongly be mistaken for 'eros' love. But in infatuation, the person has an unreasonable and obsessive admiration, or sexual passion, towards you. They are not asking your opinion if you are also interested in them. They are just crazy about you. They dream about you. They fantasise about you. Not everyone can differentiate between infatuation and love. You should therefore be careful so that you do not fall into the temptation to quickly accept the compliments of people you don't really know. Especially, when they start inviting you out, or begin to propose to you, the first time they meet you. It is possible it is in their own head!

> ***"Not everyone can differentiate between infatuation and love."***

2. Hormonal pressure

It is another factor that dictates some people's response to love. Ladies are known to feel very horny at certain times of their menstrual cycle. They can be sexually aroused at that time. This can make them quite vulnerable. They are feeling sexual urges due to an increase in oestrogen levels. The same applies to young men who are at the peak of their testosterone levels. It is hard for them to control themselves. All they are looking for is a girl to sleep with to release their sexual tension. Their desire for you may be due to hormonal pressure which makes it difficult to control themselves. After sleeping with you a few times, they may not like you again. Do not let people use you to satisfy their own sexual pleasures.

3. A recent relationship breakdown

This is also another cause of hasty proposals. When people have lost their relationship, they are more likely to seek comfort through replacement. They may not love you per se, but they may just feel sad and lonely.

Andy, 26, narrated his ordeal, "When my relationship with Amanda did not work, I felt so sad, miserable and dejected. I could not eat properly for weeks. I could not sleep, and I could not go out. I felt so depressed and lonely. A lady colleague at work started to talk to me and showed me love and comfort. She was not someone I fancied at all but there was an emotional connection within a week, so we slept together. It was the silliest mistake I made because I know her husband, but we carried on for a long time until the husband found out. As a Christian, I knew it was a sin and selfish on my part, but I was too lonely and needed some comfort."

4. Peer and age pressure

It is another reason some people may selfishly pretend they love you. All their classmates are getting married. Those who have not married have boyfriends which they parade as trophies at every gathering. There is therefore pressure on such people to find a catch as soon as possible. You dare not come near and show any interest in them; you are a catch.

Grace said, "At 27, any time I have an invitation to attend a wedding of friends or family members, my chin drops in despair. Moreso when they are younger than me, I hate it. I fear the constant barrage of questions from uncles and aunties at the wedding. They will come to you, praise you and finally they will ask the inevitable and the dreaded question. Is yours happening any time soon? I am tempted to accept any proposal from a guy whether I love him or not. This way, I can also say I am dating, and my wedding is coming soon, just to please them."

5. Visa and legal document

Some people will show interest in you not because they really love you. They are seeking for their interest and safety. They know you have the right of residence in the country of residence. They don't have one. They need to secure themselves. You are a big target. They may never disclose to you that they do not have the right to stay, until deep into the relationship when they know they have captivated your heart. **It is not wrong to marry a person without legal stay per se but be careful you are not used and abandoned.**

Eric narrated his ordeal with a young woman when he was on holiday in Accra. "When this lady I met on the beach realised that I come from London, before I came to my senses we had slept together in a hotel along the beach. Very expensive hotel. In the end, within 6 months I had married her and brought her to London. What I did not know was that she was in a long-term relationship with a guy in Accra. When I found out that she was remitting this guy, the marriage ended within a year. But I had wasted a lot of money on her. I have learnt my lesson in the hard way."

Because of poverty and lack, some countries that are considered rich countries are sought after. Young people want to use any available means, legal or illegal to get there. Once you come from such countries, you will always be a target to use to get there.

6. Just sex

You see, we live in an era where sex outside marriage is overwhelmingly popular. Many young people are keen to have sex without shame. They think it is a game. After all, everyone does it. Young Christian men and women are under enormous pressure to break their virginity before marriage.

Derek, 27, and a Christian said of a lady he was interested in from church, told him, "If you are not ready for me to try first, you must find another woman."

Derek says in the end he had to quit that relationship because he was not going to sin against his God. How many Dereks and Josephs are still out there who will place God above sex?

Be aware that not all proposals or interests are genuine. Look out for the dogs who are sniffing to take advantage of you and disappear. They will tell you they love you, but can you differentiate real love from sex love?

> ***"Be aware that not all proposals or interests are genuine."***

7. Time differentials

They look very good. They seem to have everything you would want from a spouse when you are ready. But you know too well that you are not ready to marry now. There is a big age gap between you. They are under pressure to marry now. But you are just in your first year at university. You are not sure what you want to do with your life yet. In fact, you have not even dreamt about marriage. You have not prayed about marriage. They met you just once and they are talking about marriage to you. Check the timing, please!

The offer seems good, but the timing is wrong. What do you do? What effect will this have on your study? **If the offer is good but the timing is wrong, pass! Wait for your turn.** He is not the only man or woman you have to marry. They are very mature and know what they want. They know what they are doing. But what about you?

8. You have a great job and good money

Whenever you have been blessed with a good job, it is likely the vultures and the pigs will try to dabble in them. Money and good jobs are so attractive to people. You owe yourself the duty to look well so that you can avoid the gold hunters when God has blessed you with a good job or money. My mother used to tell me, "*When you have corn in your hands, the chicks will always follow you.*" She says, "*It is difficult to know who really loves you when you have money. So be careful who you propose to and who proposes to you because of money.*"

Joseph, 35, and married his second wife a year ago said, "My first wife was 5 years older. She had a 12-year-old girl and was divorced. When she showed interest in me, I thought I was lucky. I grabbed it with both hands. She had a house and a good job. She drove her own car. Besides, she goes to church. What else do I want? I started having nightmares a month before our wedding. One elderly woman in church told me to tread cautiously but I went ahead and married her. The marriage was over two years after our wedding. I found her very controlling and manipulative. She treated me like her son. We argued over everything. It was messy. I learnt my lessons the hard way. Not all that glitters is gold."

9. Good body and shape

Beauty drives people into ditches. Some people will follow boys and girls who are well-endowed in the looks department. Even some so-called 'spirit-filled and Holy Ghost-baptised' Christians will suspend prayer and chase beauty. You must be aware of your value so that you do not fall into the wrong hands. They say they love you, but it might be just because of your beauty.

I was asking my girls why the young men of this generation are all growing beards. Apparently, all the girls now want boys who have beards and sideburns. If you also go to the gym and you are strong, you are well sought after.

The girls tell me that boys with six-packs and strong upper bodies are so attractive. Of course, everyone wants to date a person who is good-looking. But beware of external beauty alone. They can fade and fail you.

10. Kindness and generosity

This can sometimes send the wrong signal to people of the opposite sex. They may see your kindness as an invitation to love. Everyone wants to be with people who are kind. No wonder, many people would like to date you or propose to you. You must be careful when you are receiving gifts from boys or girls. They can enslave you.

11. Talent or gifts

This is an open secret that people who have talent, who are famous or in the public space get a lot of attention from opposite sexes. Are you a drummer, a great singer, or a church leader? You will be a target. Beware that not all proposals are great for you.

Charlie talks of his problem, "Since I started playing the keyboard two years ago, ten girls have approached me to go out with me. Sometimes, I feel like I am doing something wrong. I did not ask for this. I am just a little 21-year-old boy praising God with my gift. Why do I have to suffer from this?"

12. Emotionally intelligent

If you have the capacity to easily figure out what the opposite gender needs and you provide for them, this will attract suitors. In my interactions with ladies, one of the qualities they admire is men who are emotionally aware of their surroundings and offer support. They admire men who do not only hug you but say the right thing at the right time.

13. Men and women of God

Even the devil likes Mog or Wog. They may love you because you are a praying person. They may love you because you are a church leader. For that reason, they may try to influence you with gifts and attention. The question is do you also love them? As a man of God or woman of God, you must not take your marriage for granted. Do not leave it to chance. Don't take it just because they propose to you. Be intentional. Be vigilant!

GENUINE LOVE

You will be married to a man or a woman no matter how long it takes. Be careful not to waste too much time worrying about who to marry. Believe in your heart. Believe in your prayers. Believe in your spirit. Believe in your instinct. Know how God speaks to you and discern rightly when you have the urge to propose to anyone or someone who proposes to you.

Be rest assured that there are genuine God-fearing people out there who want to marry you. But be guided by the acid test for love; lack of fear in love!

> *"There is no fear in love. But perfect love drives out fear, because fear has to do with punishment. The one who fears is not made perfect in love."*
>
> 1 JOHN 4:18 NIV

CHECKPOINT

If you are in a relationship, list three reasons why you think this is not a fake love.

"As a man of God or woman of God,
you must not take your marriage for granted."

CHAPTER 17

The Sharp End of Love

When everything is going according to plan love is the sweetest feeling ever. *Why this sweet feeling does not continue forever is beyond belief.* It is a known fact that many relationships will one day end. Someone is going through it this very minute. Another person will go through this the next moment. But there are many uncountable persons who have suffered the sharp end of broken love.

When love between individuals fails, it can result in many unfavourable outcomes. This includes frustration, disappointment, rejection, feeling used and dumped, stress, depression, heartbreak and fainting episodes. The effect is felt sharply in the heart, the mind and the soul.

The pain of breaking up feels like your heart has been stabbed with a sharp, deadly sword. This is the reason why you should be careful before giving your heart to someone in the name of love. When you give your heart to someone and they reject you, it can affect your mental wellbeing. It can affect your mind. It can make you mentally deranged. It is a serious issue. Some people refuse to fall in love again. They will have the fear of getting closer to love. **But be aware that whether love fails or sticks, love can be hard work and a difficult venture.**

Peter says that love has taught him a lot of things. "I thought being single was difficult until I married one year ago. Jane and I never had any argument when we were dating. Everything seemed heavenly. But now we seem to disagree over everything. I question myself if she is the same person I married. We both want the marriage, and we are working hard to hold it together but is not easy."

> ***"But be aware that whether love fails or sticks, love can be hard work and a difficult venture."***

A. THE DEMANDS OF LOVE

If you agree to love, then you must agree to meet the demands and challenges of love. When love is sleeping it looks very innocent and harmless. But once you wake it up, you are not in control again. Love will tell you what it needs.

> *"Place me like a seal over your heart, like a seal on your arm; for love is as strong as death, its jealousy unyielding as the grave. It burns like blazing fire, like a mighty flame. Many waters cannot quench love; rivers cannot sweep it away. If one were to give all the wealth of one's house for love, it would be utterly scorned."*
>
> SONG OF SONGS 8:6-7 NIV

1. Place me like a seal over your heart

A seal is like a signet or ring-signet. It usually indicates that something or a product is original and not fake. Usually, a seal lasts a long time. More so when it is placed well in the heart and the arm. *Love works best when it is protected and secured.*

To do this, you need to place it like a seal in the heart and display it on the arm. **The first demand of love is that you must authenticate and validate me.** Make me feel original. Make me feel special. Let others see me as your only love. Keep me so close to your heart! If you are not ready to meet this demand, think again before you accept love or wake love up. Love demands to be placed on the heart as a seal. Can you tattoo the love in your heart? It is a demand. Make everyone know your heart belongs to me. My name is firmly inscribed on your heart. Make it plain and open!

"Love demands to be placed on the heart as a seal."

2. Love is as strong as death

Love is not only possessive, but also obsessive! Love is also very addictive! When you fall in love, it is so difficult to get out of it. It will consume you! Your love should be as strong as death. Death will pursue you and when it grabs you, you are dead! No one can deliver you from his hand. Mighty men have all been overcome by death. When you find a person you love, so must you be to them. Let your love grip him or her. Whatever you do for him or her to get stuck to you, please do. Let him think of you at work, sleep, wherever! Spoil her with your love so that they forget their mother!

3. Love stings

Love bites. Love burns. Love leaves a mark where it goes. You will see it. You will also feel it. Your partner will do the same. People you have no love for do not mean much to you. But you will get hurt and offended by the same people you love. If you are afraid to be stung like a bee by love, it is probably better you stay out of love.

4. Love is jealous

People fight in marriage because someone spoke to their ex-boyfriend or girlfriend. If you are not prepared to forsake all and love that person, it will be difficult to be in a relationship. Once you have chosen him or her to be your love, please close one of your eyes and focus on them alone.

5. Love is fire

Love is a flame. Love's flame is mighty. Love burns. Love's flame is unquenchable. When love gets hold of you, you will feel the heat. If it is a flame, the people around you feel its heat! Demonstrate your love with passion! No amount of water can quench it. You will call for all the fire tanks in the country, but I am afraid the heat will be on. When you are not ready, let love sleep.

"Demonstrate your love with passion."

6. Love is unyielding

You must be stubborn with your love. You must be resolute! You don't buckle under pressure! You don't give in to pressure. You are not swayed by anyone or anything.

You are not walking away from this beautiful wife, this handsome man, these amazing kids and this fine home. You will die to keep this family intact. You will work hard to keep this love. You will work hard to protect this family. You work with your sweat and blood, soul and spirit to make this marriage work. This is the power of love!

In Songs of Songs, the lady is demanding the same. If you really love me that much, if I mean so much to you, then you should not give up. Love is unyielding like a grave. It does not let their victims go. That should be your mind-set, once you get married. If you feel you are going to have a taster session in marriage, think twice. There might not be a way out!

B. ATTACHMENT TO LOVE IS PAINFUL

One of the reasons why couples think they are not feeling love is that emotions and feelings fade away with time. This happens when we come to live together, to adapt and attach to each other.

Psychologists believe that before we fall in love, we first lust after them. We get attracted to them. Then we are attached to them. Attachment can be abrasive and uncomfortable. There might be a period of repulsion and a feeling of rejection. This can lead to a reduction in positive feelings towards your mate.

Scientists also believe that the positive feelings in romance during love, deactivate the neural pathway responsible for negative emotions such as fear and social judgment. When we are involved in romantic love, the neural machinery responsible for making critical assessments of other people, including critical assessments of those with whom we are romantically involved, shuts down.

That is the neural basis for ancient wisdom, "LOVE IS BLIND." Hormone levels are never the same in anyone. They fluctuate during the day. They decline over the years as well. Anything controlled by hormones will never remain the same with time!

But during attachment, when couples are closer each day, seeing their weaknesses all the time, and expectations unmet in the relationship, this can lead to criticism, resentment, unhappiness and reduction in affection. This is the reason why the feeling of love will not last forever.

Richard, 31, says, "When I met Cyndy, I thought we were made in heaven. The chemistry between us was something I had never felt before. I couldn't sleep. I couldn't eat if I hadn't seen her. Fast forward, six months later, attraction has faded. I still love her, but I don't want to see her every day."

Some less mature people will be quick to break the relationship. They think they are not attracted to each other and hence they are not in love anymore. Be careful you do not let love go so easily. It might just be the natural fading or more attachment causing your negative feelings towards them.

There are hormones involved as well. Love loses its power when the dopamine levels begin to fade. The feeling of love will also fade. Scientists believe that oxytocin and vasopressin regulate bonding with mates, feelings of contentment, calmness and security. The action of these two hormones explains why passionate love fades as attachment grows.

> ***"Love loses its power when the dopamine levels begin to fade."***

C. FEAR OF LOVE

I have come across a few individuals who are afraid of falling in love for a few reasons. Such a phenomenon is called **philophobia.**

Such people have had unpleasant experiences. Some of the fears are justified. Others are based on hearsay or other people's narratives. Children brought up in bad homes may be put off by love and marriage. Some parents' pains and hurts are picked up by their children.

When people have suffered abuse and mistreatment in their various homes, they shudder when they hear the word love.

Such people paint love as not worth all the effort. Dan says he has not been lucky in two relationships. Both ended bizarrely and left him broken-hearted. He says even if God dropped an angel from heaven, he would not date her.

He said "I am done with relationships. I am not lucky. Maybe God does not want me to marry. I have accepted that. In fact, I am too scared to go near any woman."

Bad relationships or broken relationships can leave you so traumatised that you might not want to date again. This is why it is important to take your time to fall in love with the right person at the right time.

> ***"This is why it is important to take your time to fall in love with the right person at the right time."***

D. HAVE YOUR OWN EXPERIENCE

When I was growing up, I did not see my parents sitting together to enjoy each other. My parents talked to each other. I thought that was how marriage worked. I never liked to go home or around my parents. Luckily, I did not have to live with them for a long time. I was always living with other families.

But when I became grounded in the Lord, and the word of God had access to my heart, my perspective changed. I appreciated the correct definition of love. I saw the character and behaviour of love. I also saw how love is demonstrated. From that time onwards, I knew I was ready to love the right way.

My friend Frank used to say, "If you don't know what good is like, whatever you see is good for you." I decided that I would marry and marry well. I said my marriage would be better than my parents. Indeed, I got married to Phyllis over 25 years ago. Our marriage is not perfect, but we enjoy each other's company. Having a new understanding of love through the word of God changed everything for me.

Marriage is hard, but yours could be different if you are ready to invest in your relationship. There are more people, who make no noise about their marriage, as they are enjoying it. Make your own experience. You are different from your parents or friends. You will not marry the same person as them.

Your story could be different. Do not let fear cripple your love. As a believer, you have an abundance of good love or godly love in you. All you need to do is to ensure that you find the right person who deserves it and shower them with your unquenchable love.

The Bible has said there is no fear in love. It should be your watchword. When you are going out with someone and you begin to fear, please pause and pray. Hear from God before you proceed.

CHECKPOINT

When you marry, how comfortable will you be able to display your spouse in public places and among your friends and family?

"Marriage is hard, but yours could be different if you are ready to invest in your relationship."

SECTION FIVE

THE CHRISTIAN GUIDE TO DATING

CHAPTER 18

Courtship, Arranged Marriages and Dating

"It is the same way with dating. The time you are most prepared for dating is when you don't need anyone to complete you, fulfil you, or instil in you a sense of worth or purpose."

MYLES MUNROE

Many Christian singles struggle regarding what to do and what not to do during the dating or courtship period. This section will help you date in a godly manner and with confidence.

I will discuss traditional or cultural dating, secular or contemporary dating, and Christ-centred dating. I will also discuss the good and the ugly part of dating, and finally, what to do if your dating relationship breaks down

IS COURTSHIP OLD SCHOOL?

It was 4 pm at the dinner table on Sunday, after we had enjoyed my wife's amazing dinner for the family. A conversation popped up about relationships. I was asked how long it took for Phyllis and I to marry after meeting.

All three of my children, and other young couples in their 30s were present. I had the shock of my life. There was an explosion of laughter from all of them, except my wife and another friend, who were both in their 50s. What was my crime? I told them that the courtship between Phyllis and I lasted two and a half years before we married. What set them off was the use of the term 'courtship'.

My second daughter, who was then 18 years old, taught me something new that day. She said, "*Dad, you must not use the term 'courtship' on any platform. It is not cool. It is so outdated, and no one uses that term anymore.*" I felt so humbled by my own children, and the youth present.

As a speaker, I must be seen to be abreast with the current trend. So, I decided to do a little digging into the two terms.

WHAT THEN IS COURTSHIP?

A simple definition of courtship is "one man and one woman spending intentional time together to get to know each other with the expressed purpose of evaluating the other as a potential husband or wife" – Wikipedia.

The main aim of courtship is to take time to study each other either from afar or close, for suitability in marriage. You are listening, watching and observing if this person is good for you. It usually means both of you live in the same community. This courtship process varies from culture to culture.

Before the sexual revolution in Europe and in America, courtship did not include sexual intimacy. It was not a time of kissing or caressing each other. It was a serious time for observing, appreciating and checking suitability, or compatibility.

In the days of strict Western society, chaperones were required when dates had been arranged. Chaperones were usually members of your family, such as your mother or aunt, who would accompany you on your date to ensure everything was above board. The Chinese would do it differently, as well as the Africans and Indians.

My mother told me when she was going out with my father, she didn't need anyone to keep an eye on them. Because they were not Christians, she fell pregnant in the process before the marriage. Dating was very difficult for many young people back then, just as it is today! People are unable to control themselves and eventually end up having sexual intercourse.

I also observed in my tradition growing up that many couples were cohabiting even before they performed the marriage rights. This is the reason why many people favour arranged marriages. No courtship. No temptation. No hassle. If you agree to marry, you do it now, a quick and easy way to marry.

> *"The main aim of courtship is to take time to study each other either from afar or close, for suitability in marriage."*

ARRANGED MARRIAGES WORKED WELL

Even though many youths in today's world frown upon arranged marriages, it served its purpose well in those times, and even now in many cultures. *Almost all marriages in the biblical times were arranged and there was no such thing as courtship, no wonder this terminology is not found in the Bible.*

Parents and families took the hassle from their young people. After all, they knew better than them. They can tell a better woman or man from the lot. They would investigate the background of potential suitors behind the scenes, ensuring they were members of the community with good standing. No chronic diseases, psychological condition or bad name in the family. Finally, they ensured that the man had the capacity to look after the woman. He had to have a stable job and a source of income, possibly a farm or office job.

It worked very well due to the dynamics at the time. Men and women lived a very simple lifestyle and communities were closer to each other. Men were usually the main breadwinners. Life was simple and full of contentment. No TV, no cars, no aeroplanes, no mortgages, no taxes and no internet. The most important requirements were food, shelter and clothing.

Women were more interested in men who would provide them with security, food, clothing and children. Women did not have the strength to do this for themselves. Work was tedious and laborious. If any man provided this for you, they were your hero. Marriage was not about love or friendship. It was about meeting your basic needs. Ladies married quite young, so it was important for parents and family members to decide the best husband for them.

Even today, many cultures in Africa, the Middle East, Asia and China practise arranged marriages. *One recent study found that 70% of all Indian marriages in this dispensation are arranged and do not offer the couples a chance to court or date.*

In certain cultures, in Africa, the man must abduct the woman and run away with her. He later comes back with the lady and performs the marriage rites. He is considered strong and a hero if he can do that. There is no wooing, if the woman agrees to marry you, that is your chance! Just find your moment and secretly run away with her! Usually in the night when everyone is sleeping. This was their way of courtship. This is still practised. Today, going out still varies from culture to culture. The Westerners call it dating, which is different from courtship.

WHY COURTSHIP AND ARRANGED MARRIAGES ARE LESS POPULAR

One major reason for the decline in the courtship and arranged systems is the beginning of the Industrial Revolution, which created many jobs that suited the modern-day woman. Women have their own money to look after themselves. Women are leading countries and corporations due to their higher levels of education. They make their own choices today. They buy their own food, cars and even houses. Women's education means that women do not marry as young as they used to. By the time they want to settle down and marry after university, they are usually old enough to make their own choices.

This era is possibly the best time for women who now select their own husbands. It is fun. It is liberating. But it can also be scary. You now have all the men in the world to choose from, thanks to the almighty internet. If you are a person who loves fun, you have the world at your feet. No limit as to what, and where, you and your date can go. Going out for entertainment, restaurants, church and holidays is so easy and accessible. It usually poses more problems for the spirit-filled Christian who wants to avoid premarital sex!

THE PRESSURE AND FUN OF DATING

Unfortunately, with the turn of the century, the meaning of dating has shifted drastically. Dating in Western and contemporary societies is a period of fun and entertainment. It is now commonplace for sexual fulfilment when young people say they are dating or going out.

For too many people it is just a period where teens, adolescents and single adults go out for fun. What fun means is subject to the individuals involved, but we know that they go out to eat, attend parties, drink, and even have sex. Loneliness in today's world has provided harsh conditions for young people who may not go out to play all week. They are lonely, bored, and stressed.

Everyone needs love, acceptance and affection. Whether you are in your 20s or 70s, when you realise that you feel lonely, you will start checking to find who is available to chat or date. Some people will resort to dating apps or online dating for companionship. Others will use the telephone or social media to connect with friends and lovers.

Many young singles, adult singles, divorced, divorcees, widows, widowers, and sadly many others who are married, look for love to date. Did I say married people look for dates? Yes, some do!

In 2019, Ashley Maddison, an online dating service that provides a platform for married couples to date people who are not their partners celebrated a milestone of a whopping 60 million membership! In 2025, the figure will be way higher. It is difficult to say if some Christians also participate in Ashley Madison services, but we know that both Christians and non-Christians cheat on their spouses. Essentially, this platform is proud of helping married couples to have affairs or cheat! Do you know their motto? "Life is short have an affair."

No wonder that recent study has found that 50% of youth have sex in their first month of dating! If your aim is to study someone to marry them, technically, that is courtship, and this is a serious matter! I will show you the differences between courting and dating.

	Courtship	Dating
Meeting place	Private	Public
Structure	Yes	More flexible
Motive	Marriage	Fun
Duration	1-3 years	No time
Initiators	Friends, family, church	Selves
Seriousness	Very serious	Not serious
Commitment	Yes	No
Family	Very involved	Not necessary
Parental Consent	Required	Not required
Abstinence	Yes	No
Emotional attachment	Fast	Slow or not required
Monogamous	Yes	May or may not
Accountability	Too many stakeholders	None
Taking lead	Male	Male or female

CHECKPOINT

Compare the dating of your parents to yours today. List three things you think are better now than theirs.

"Everyone needs love, acceptance and affection."

CHAPTER 19

Guide to Christian Dating

"Be ye therefore followers of God, as dear children; and walk in love, as Christ also hath loved us, and hath given himself for us an offering and a sacrifice to God for a sweet-smelling savour. But fornication, and all uncleanness, or covetousness, let it not be once named among you, as becometh saints."

EPHESIANS 5:1-3 KJV

The world has changed quite a great deal since the time Phyllis and I were dating, probably courting as we used to call it. As a church boy through and through, I could not be seen walking hand in hand with her. I had to be clean before God and man. I used to preach in the church, on the street, and campuses, advising the youth to flee from sexual immorality. All that time, I never had a girlfriend, so it was not difficult for me until I met this very beautiful lady, who is now my wife. Then I realised that it was easier said than done.

But the church and the Bible have rules and expectations for young singles during dating. I could be suspended if I was found to have broken those rules. My marriage may not have been blessed, nor given the honour and the fanfare that comes with it. I could have been embarrassed and ashamed. My reputation as a youth leader, and as a presbyter, was on the line. Phyllis and I agreed that we had a lot to protect, so we would not engage in sexual activity until we were fully married. We prayed constantly for the strength of God to go through that period. Let me be frank here, it was not easy at all. To be around a person you are so attracted to romantically yet having to delay your pleasures for future enjoyment was hard. But we agreed not to sin against God and our own bodies, just like Joseph did.

> *"No one is greater in this house than I am.*
> *My master has withheld nothing from me except you,*
> *because you are his wife. How then could I do such*
> *a wicked thing and sin against God?"*
>
> GENESIS 39:9 NIV

But I can report that to God be the glory, we were able to overcome this temptation.

There is a BIG difference between secular dating and Christian dating. While there may not be any restrictions or requirements in secular dating, there are requirements and expectations of Christian youth or singles when they are dating. It is not about the church. It is not about your parents. Christianity is not mere words. It is not about the tongues you speak. It is about your respect and obedience to God. *It is about doing what God is expecting of you as a true believer! The Word of God says, "… By this you shall know them…" It is not the words. It is the FRUIT!*

In Christian dating, prospective couples are not only accountable to the church, but they must also prove their salvation with fear and trembling.

> *"Therefore, my dear friends, as you have always obeyed, not only in my presence but now much more in my absence, continue to work out your own salvation with fear and trembling."*
>
> PHILIPPIANS 2:12 NIV

I admit the world has corrupted the real meaning and purpose of dating. This has unfortunately affected the way many believers behave during dating. Many young Christians are dating without Christ in it. They are dating without the fear of God. They are dating the same way their ungodly friends do. This is very disappointing.

One of my trusted nieces told me, "Uncle, these youths you see jumping in church and speaking in tongues are sleeping with their boyfriends and girlfriends. This is because it seems acceptable that if you love the boys, you must sleep with them. Otherwise, they leave for another girl who compromises."

This situation is concerning. Christians must understand they are different and must date differently. What then is godly dating?

> ***"It is about doing what God is expecting of you as a true believer! It is not the words. It is the FRUIT!"***

ARE CHRISTIANS DATING OR COURTING?

Godly dating or courting depending on which generation you grew up in, is a period when single or young adults, male and female go out, with the aim of studying each other, so that they can become husband and wives as soon as possible in a godly way. To be honest, whether you call it courtship or dating is irrelevant. What is important is that you both acknowledge God in your interaction.

If you are going out to drink alcohol, walk in dark places and even sleep together, you have taken Christ out of your relationship. This is secular dating. Two Christians dating does not make your dating Christian. Christ never dated. The Apostles never dated. There is no recommendation in the Bible to date your potential spouse. ***If your dating reflects Christ, then it is Christian dating. It is what you do in your dating that matters not who is doing the dating.***

Regardless of your spirituality, this period is usually marked with excitement and anticipation. You are madly in love with a boy or girl, and you cannot wait to go out with them just like any unbeliever feels. Your whole body and emotions are intoxicated with good feelings, just by the sound of their voices. Your sleeping time is getting shorter. When you have not heard from them, you are getting agitated. Even if you come from a strict family, you will look for every reason under the universe, usually lies, just to get out to meet them. Love has found you! That is the reality of relationships.

Meghan says "Since Jessie and I started going out, I hardly have enough sleep for myself. We speak on phone until 3 am. Sometimes I forget I must wake up at 6 am to catch a train to work. I am sleep deprived. But you know what, it does not bother me at all. It is so fun to be in love with Jessie."

Many young people will go through a few dates before settling on Mr or Mrs Right. But some young people will be very lucky to just marry the first person they dated.

Matt and Nancy are married for 2 years now. They are both 28 years old. Nancy said, "Marrying Matt is the best thing that happened to me. He rescued me from unholy relationships. I had kissed several frogs before I met him. I will advise young people never to rush into a relationship just because friends are doing it."

Young people are rushing into dating due to peer pressure. They feel left out. They feel they are missing out on fun. That means anyone who shows up, is a good catch. Be intentional and be ready for the type of person you want to marry. Let's look at what you must do when you are dating

FIVE ULTIMATE GUIDES FOR GODLY DATING

1. Date as Friends

Many people give themselves away before their parents meet this person. There is no honour to you, your parents or Christ when you give yourself away before your parents have the chance to do so. This is one of the biggest issues in contemporary dating. **Christ-centred dating should be devoid of marital duties. You are not married, do not give yourself away!**

Both parties must be clear and agree to follow the process leading to marriage. Behave as godly friends who are attracted to each other. You are however prepared to wait to be properly married and blessed by the church, your parents and ultimately by God!

2. Date with a Date in Mind

Do not date aimlessly just for the fun of it. Some people enter relationships when they are not ready. They date for eternity. Christian dating is different from secular dating. **Christians do not date just for fun; we date with the end goal of marriage!**

If he or she does not have an idea of when you can marry, the chance is that it is not the right time or right person for you.

Claire said, "Ken and I started dating when we were in secondary school year 12. I was 16 years old and he was 17 years old. I am now 23 but he says he is not ready to marry. We have broken many promises we made to each other. I feel we have wasted each other's time for nothing. My advice to young people especially, Christians is that do not rush into a relationship until you are close to marriage."

Temptations are real. The more time you spend in a relationship, the higher the chance of falling into sexual sin. **My recommendation is not to enter a relationship until you are ready to marry in the next three years at most.**

3. Date with Both Eyes Open

Dating should offer you the chance to be closer to the person. People you meet at church may be different when you meet them at home. What are they like when you are alone with them? When they are driving their car in traffic, how calm are they? When you visit them, how tidy are they? How is this person's relationship with their parents and siblings?

You must not date with your eyes closed. Open both eyes now and when married shut one of them.

We all have one psychological condition or another. Look out for such conditions which may be subtle or glaring.

Felix says, "I knew I had something, but I didn't know what it was. I can be happy for four weeks. Then two weeks following, I am a wretch. This became worse when I started dating Patricia. I would go weeks without returning her call. But she persisted. We got married one year ago. It became too much for us that we asked for psychological and psychiatry interventions. I have now been diagnosed with bipolar disorder. I can see Pat is disappointed for not knowing this but she says, at least she can be more patient to support me."

There are several psychological and neurological conditions, including **Attention Deficit Hyperactivity Disorder (ADHD), Obsessive-Compulsive Disorder (OCD)**, Asperger's Disease and many more. They are common neurodevelopmental disorders in children. It is usually first diagnosed in childhood and often lasts into adulthood. It is not anyone's fault. People are helped or trained to lead their normal lives. But in extreme cases, living with such people can be a bit challenging. You need patience and love to live with people who have these conditions. If you feel it is not for you, maybe, it will be better to end the relationship.

> **"You must not date with your eyes closed. Open both eyes now and when married shut one of them."**

4. Look Out for Enduring Qualities

> *"Love is patient and kind. Love is not jealous or boastful or proud or rude. It does not demand its own way. It is not irritable, and it keeps no record of being wronged. It does not rejoice about injustice but rejoices whenever the truth wins out. Love never gives up, never loses faith, is always hopeful, and endures through every circumstance."*
>
> 1 CORINTHIANS 13:4-7 NLT

Many physical attributes you see in this person will not always remain. Even if it does, when you see it all the time, the attraction may reduce considerably. What will keep your love going is not that nice beard, it will not be the six-pack, it will not be the nice hair or long legs. What will keep your marriage going, will be those enduring qualities that never fail.

If she says she loves you, does she give up on you or have patience with you? If he says he loves you, does he let things go, or does he keep a record of wrongs? This is what brought Josh and Helen together.

"Josh is a peacemaker. He does not dwell on people's weaknesses. I realised this long ago even before we started going out. He is also gentle and patient. Same qualities have shone through our marriage," says Helen.

In difficult times in your marriage, it is these enduring principles and qualities demonstrated that will determine the longevity of your marriage.

5. Affirm Their Great Qualities

People do better when their good deeds are spoken back to them. Contrary to what people say, you must also look out for the great qualities this person has and let them know how that makes you happy. Your aim is to provide feedback. When you give them positive feedback, they are more likely to listen and amend their ways, if possible, than on your not-so-pleasant feedback.

> *"In difficult times in your marriage,*
> *it is these enduring principles and qualities*
> *demonstrated that will determine the*
> *longevity of your marriage."*

CHECKPOINT

Everyone has their own values or family values that guide them during dating. List three personal values that guide you during dating.

"Love is patient and kind. Love is not jealous or boastful or proud or rude."

CHAPTER 20

Rules and Conduct of Christian Dating

Dating has always been a big challenge for young Christians. At this time in their lives, they are filled with sexual energy. Young men are at the peak of their testosterone levels. This is the hormone that controls masculinity. They have high sexual passion. The females are also the same. They have high levels of oestrogen which is the female's sexual hormone. It is like petrol and fire if you dare put them in a room where there's nobody around them!

To avoid this happening is hard for any young couple. Some with the help of the Holy Spirit pass this test without any sexual activity. But many fail miserably! Christian churches have a responsibility to encourage, direct and guide young people who are going out.

They should not be suspected of doing anything evil, if we have had time to educate them on their duty as Christians, to be pure and holy in all their endeavours. This section is aimed at helping you to date with confidence and protecting your integrity as a believer without shame and regret.

1. DATE A BELIEVER

> *"Do not be yoked together with unbelievers. For what do righteousness and wickedness have in common? Or what fellowship can light have with darkness?"*
>
> 2 CORINTHIANS 6:14 NIV

This has been a long-held biblical principle and tradition. Is it true in our time? Why can't I marry anyone I like? It is still true, even though you can still marry anyone you choose if you are not a Christian.

Abi, 38, a Christian and a daughter of a pastor decided to marry a man who was agnostic. Abi says "I thought all I needed at the time was love. We are four siblings. My dad was always busy with his ministry in London. We literally ran the home because my mom was always working. I did not feel my parents' love. So, when Jeff said he loved me, I did not care what religion he was into. We are still together after five years but I am not happy that every Sunday I go to church with my son alone. He doesn't believe in prayer, so I do that for my son and him, which I miss from my parents' home. It is not ideal to be in my position. It is difficult but I am married."

It is possible Abi may be able to win Jeff for Christ later. But it is hard work. Marriage is hard enough even between two spirit-filled believers. Marrying a person who does not share your faith is even more difficult. Besides, you want a husband or a wife you can see in heaven. Loving someone who will love you in Christ makes a lot of difference.

2. PROVE TO EACH OTHER YOU ARE BORN AGAIN

> *"By their fruit you will recognize them. Do people pick grapes from thornbushes, or figs from thistles?"*
> MATTHEW 7:16 NIV

Words are cheap but actions are the real deal. Praying and singing in church is easy and anyone can do it. You will prove your faith and obedience by what you do with your boyfriend or girlfriend, especially in private. It is easy to profess to be a man, or woman, of God in public. What is the evidence? In the words of our Lord and Saviour Jesus Christ, "*...by their fruit, you shall know those who are truly Christians.*" Let your fruit show that you are a Mog or a Wog.

> ***"Marriage is hard enough even between two spirit-filled believers."***

3. PRIORITISE PURITY AND HOLINESS

> *"It is God's will that you should be sanctified: that you should avoid sexual immorality; that each of you should learn to control your own body in a way that is holy and honourable, not in passionate lust like the pagans, who do not know God; and that in this matter no one should wrong or take advantage of a brother or sister. The Lord will punish all those who commit such sins, as we told you and warned you before. For God did not call us to be impure, but to live a holy life."*
> 1 THESSALONIANS 4:3-7 NIV

Sexual immorality can have a very negative effect on you as a Christian. It does not only make you unholy, it separates you from God. It also blocks your prayer! God wants sex to take place in marriage. Young persons should reserve sexual intimacy until they are married. This is in honour of God. It is also proof of your obedience and integrity in Christ.

If you are pressured by your boyfriend or girlfriend to have sex when dating or courting, you must ask yourself if you are in the right relationship.

4. DO NOT CONFORM

> *"Do not conform to the pattern of this world,*
> *but be transformed by the renewing of your mind.*
> *Then you will be able to test and approve what*
> *God's will is—his good, pleasing and perfect will."*
>
> ROMANS 12:2 NIV

The world is trying to influence and dilute Christianity. The new paradigm is that *you do what is good for you.* They will say it to your face you are missing out if you do not follow their pattern. This is where you and your boyfriend, or girlfriend, must resist them fiercely.

You must ensure that you do not become their convert. **A person without the word of God and the Holy Spirit finds it difficult to be disciplined and holy. They will also lack self-control.** But you as a child of God, are blessed with the gift of self-control and discipline. You can say no to sin. You must not conform to the world.

> *"Do not love the world or anything in the world.*
> *If anyone loves the world, love for the Father*
> *is not in them."*
>
> 1 JOHN 2:15 NIV

If you conform you have your reward. That reward will be a momentary pleasure. A recent popular online couple assessment survey by Relate, a relationship counselling organisation, found that the longer a dating couple waits to have sex, the better their relationship is after marriage. In fact, couples who wait until marriage to have sex report higher relationship satisfaction (20% higher), better communication patterns (12% better), less consideration of divorce (22% lower), and better sexual quality (15% better), than those who started having sex early in their dating.

For me, this is a game changer. Delay your pleasure for a better marriage!

> ***"You can say no to sin. You must not conform to the world."***

5. KEEP OPEN COMMUNICATION AND BOUNDARIES

> *"Therefore each of you must put off falsehood*
> *and speak truthfully to your neighbour,*
> *for we are all members of one body."*
>
> EPHESIANS 4:25 NIV

Being honest and open to each other will help you to be on the same page. To do that, you must communicate your preferences. You must communicate your boundaries. Speak truthfully and honestly to each other.

Jaden, 29, married to Maria for 3 years, said, "As soon as we realised, we were attracted to each other, we sat down and talked. Initially, I found it hard because I did not know what Maria was thinking, and I did not want to hurt her feelings either. I was so happy when she said, 'I was thinking the same, that we should not be kissing or touching each other to inflame passions.' By the grace of God, we kept our promises until we married. It has given us belief and trust in each other completely. Maria is not stressed when I am out there with lady friends and colleagues. She trusts I will not do anything silly."

6. BE OPEN TO MENTORSHIP

> *"Listen to advice and accept discipline, and at the end you will be counted among the wise."*
>
> PROVERBS 19:20 NIV

It helps a lot if you both agree to be mentored by experienced couples, or friends, already married. You will benefit greatly if you choose them and make them aware of your desire for them to take you under their wings.

Make regular visits to their homes. Ask them the questions that are on your mind. Be vulnerable before them. Show interest in their family. Find a chore to do for them to enable you to draw closer to them. When you are visiting it is a great idea to be generous. Find something to buy for them. It is a sign of your maturity.

Peter and Esther one of my favourite couples who recently married did that. They were so open to Phyllis and me. They visited our home every Sunday. Esther would help my wife in the kitchen whilst Peter helped me to build my shed office. They did that until they got married. This afforded us the opportunity to mentor them and be a part of their marriage.

By doing that, it makes you accountable to them, and to yourselves. It prevents you from hiding in your rooms and learning nothing. Your marriage may be different from theirs, but it gives you a head start. Do not ignore their counsel and the experiences they share with you.

7. FIND TIME TO PRAY TOGETHER

Learn to pray together when you are dating. **If you do not let prayer become a priority, the chance is that you will become more physical and sexual. The only way for both of you to avoid sexual temptation is to be spiritual!**

If you start praying together, it will be easier to pray when you are finally married. Ann and Sam are married for two years. When they came to see me, it was about one thing. Ann was upset that Sam was not showing spiritual leadership at home.

"He does not call for prayer. When I call for prayer, he would not open his mouth in prayer. Sam says he prays in his head, but this is frustrating for me because I always wanted a praying man and a spiritual leader at home."

When I asked Sam why he does not pray, he said he was brought up as a Catholic and was not taught to pray loudly. When I asked Ann if she was aware Sam was Catholic, she said yes, but did not know what their praying style was like. I asked again if they had prayed at the time of dating, and she said, no. *"But as a Pentecostal, I love to pray and be led by my husband,"* said Ann.

Ladies, if you know you would love your husband to be a spiritual leader, please test them before you marry. Ensure he loves prayer, and he will be your spiritual head. If you don't, you may be disappointed after the marriage. You cannot give what you don't have!

> ***"If you start praying together, it will be easier to pray when you are finally married."***

8. STUDY THE WORD

> *"How can a young person stay on the path of purity? By living according to your word. I seek you with all my heart; do not let me stray from your commands. I have hidden your word in my heart that I might not sin against you."*
>
> PSALMS 119:9-11 NIV

If you study the word, whilst dating, it will draw you closer to God and to each other spiritually. The word has the sanctifying power to cleanse and wash you. Set time to read the word and study it to show yourselves approved as a true man and woman of God!

> *"Study to shew thyself approved unto God, a workman that needeth not to be ashamed, rightly dividing the word of truth."*
>
> 2 TIMOTHY 2:15 KJV

As a husband, you would be required to wash and cleanse your wife with the word of God. If you do not have the word of God within you and if you do not study the word, how will you sanctify your wife?

> *"Husbands, love your wives, even as Christ also loved the church, and gave himself for it; that he might sanctify and cleanse it with the washing of water by the word."*
>
> EPHESIANS 5:25-26 KJV

If you don't want your wife to become contaminated, begin to take the word of God seriously. **If you are a woman dating a man, you must not just be interested in going out. You must demand he studies the word of God with you.**

Mark, 25, says, "The first thing I ask Linda when she calls or messages me is, what did you learn from the Bible today? Can you share it with me? This opens the gateway for insightful and inspiring discussion. We have done this for the last 12 months. I find it so helpful because it eventually takes your mind off any physicality."

When you study the word while dating, this will become your springboard and benchmark for future success in devotion as a couple.

> ***"The word has the sanctifying power to cleanse and wash you."***

9. FOCUS ON BUILDING FRIENDSHIP

> *"A friend loves at all times, and a brother is born for a time of adversity."*
>
> PROVERBS 17:17 NIV

The pinnacle of any marriage relationship is where the couple becomes not just close friends, but intimate friends. When dating, spend quality time building both emotional and spiritual support for each other. Ensure you are on a path of becoming each other's great friends. Build understanding, respect and caring relationships that will endure.

Life is very stressful after the wedding. If the two of you are not friends already, it may be difficult for you in the initial stage which can cause friction in the marriage.

Alberta and Malcom came to see me recently. Malcom is seething that Alberta is not spending time with him, nor speaking to him often.

He said, "What pisses me off is not the fact that Alberta does not speak to me, it is about how she is constantly on the phone to her mother. What about me? Who do I also talk to?"

But Alberta disagreed:

"Malcom works 60 hours a week. I do 30 hours a week. He is never at home. He forgets we were not friends before we married. He went back to work two days after our wedding. He claims he must make up for the cost of the wedding even though we shared the cost. I am not happy. I am home alone. My mother is my only friend. She is the one who encourages me. Without her, I would have gone back to my parents."

Ensure that there is no fear in your relationship. Keep each other confident and ensure that you are happy to be around each other. Defend and protect them in this period. Ensure they are comfortable around you, your friends and your family, especially your parents.

10. PASS YOUR TEMPTATION

> *"No temptation has overtaken you except what is common to mankind. And God is faithful; he will not let you be tempted beyond what you can bear. But when you are tempted, he will also provide a way out so that you can endure it."*
>
> 1 CORINTHIANS 10:13 NIV

Dating can be tempting especially for young people. It is full of temptation to commit fornication. Passing your temptation during your dating brings glory to God. It proves that not only your spouse can trust you, but God can also trust you and entrust you with bigger things. Heavens will rejoice. and angels will minister to you! Jesus has laid the template for us. When He passed his temptation; angels came to minister to him.

> *"Then the devil left him, and angels came and attended him."*
>
> MATTHEW 4:11 NIV

Maria says, "if there was one thing that I am proud of in life up to now, it is when Desmond and I were dating. He is touchy and cuddly. I had to constantly remind him of our commitment to each other and God. It felt like two years of intense trial. There were days I pretended to be sick to avoid him visiting me because I knew my flesh was demanding and I would not pass. I am proud of this achievement as we had a beautiful wedding and are now blessed with two children. I have no guilt nor regrets!"

This is awesome! Maria and her husband made heaven glad. Angels are still celebrating and ministering to them! You will also be celebrated in the same way. But you must first pass this test!

Many marriages are struggling, not because couples are not trying hard enough. It is because even though they call themselves Christians their relationship before marriage was marred by sexual sins, dishonour of parents, disrespect to the body of Christ and total disregard for God.

If you pass, God will honour your marriage! It is worth it. It is rewarding!

CHECKPOINT

List five rules and conducts you have set for yourself while dating.

"Ensure that there is no fear in your relationship."

CHAPTER 21

The Ugly Side of Dating – Red Flags

"Dating is really hard because everyone puts on a front. It's really difficult to see who is who, so it is important to be yourself."

BROOKE BURKE

You have just read about the good and the fun side of dating. But will it be fun all the time? Definitely not! Whilst many people have had no bad experiences in dating, others have suffered horrific and ugly injuries to their bodies, heart and mind. This is because some people will lie to you. Others have their own ulterior motives which you wouldn't be aware of.

Dating is indeed hard! When people know what you would not like to see, they will use their blood to cover all the red flags. They can hide the evidence. It becomes your duty to find and assess the evidence to prove they are who they say they are, or not. You haven't got a wife or husband until you have just taken your vows and come off the altar! So, take your investigation seriously!

The following are some of the most important red flags and deceptions you should be aware of and not fall for.

WHEN THERE IS PHYSICAL AND EMOTIONAL ABUSE

I have seen singles who are in a relationship that are so close to hell, but they still accept it thinking it shall be well one day.

Joyce confided in her friend that she did not know if the way her boyfriend talked down to her, exposing her in public, was normal. Jane said it was not right and that she should not put up with it. Joyce continued that there are instances where Steve has slapped her and called her names. She said she could not leave as he paid for her rent.

You are more important than money to pay for your rent or anything else. No one should accept emotional or physical abuse in any relationship.

Abuse lowers your self-esteem and destroys your confidence. You should not just refuse it; you must run away from anyone who does not respect you.

WHEN YOU ARE CONSTANTLY ARGUING AND CRITICISING EACH OTHER

Constant criticism and arguments are not just bad, but they are unhealthy for any relationship. In fact, they are a huge source of serious conflict in marriage.

No two human beings will agree on everything all the time. That will not happen. However, if your argument and criticism are becoming a regular thing in your relationship, both of you must sit back and reflect if you want this to lead to marriage. Be aware that every person has great abilities and potential, if you decide to open your eyes and see it. Constant argument and criticism are signs that you don't appreciate them and what they carry. This can be a red flag.

WHEN THEY NEVER APPRECIATE YOUR GIFTS NOR ENCOURAGE YOU

If your boyfriend or girlfriend shows no interest in your gifts and beauty or encourages you about your dreams and aspirations, it will be a problem when you marry. Marriage is not just cooking for your husband or paying the rent. Married couples are the number one fan of each other. They are each other's cheerleader! Great couples support each other's dreams, goals, ministry, and even their jobs.

When I write any script, the first reader is my wife. If she says, "What is this, Darling?", I know straight away, it is not good for consumption, and I bin it!

Fatima said to me, "Papa, all that makes my boyfriend happy is when I earn more money. When I am talking about new opportunities, he is not interested. When I am feeling down, he has no words of comfort. I am thinking, maybe he loves me because of the money I earn as a Band 7 nurse in London."

USING YOU AS SEXUAL HEALING FOR THEM

Relationship breakdown is not new. It happens all the time. The trouble is the emotional traumas and confusion that cleave to the people involved. It can leave you with depression, sadness, and even sometimes go as far as suicidal tendencies. Breaking attachment with someone who claims to love you is hard. People who are coming from a broken relationship would claim to love you so that they can sleep with you, only to heal their broken hearts. This is a red flag!

Listen to this, at least 58% of people are likely to engage in rebound sex after a break-up to try and get over their exes, according to research by Live Science.

Be alert and look out for people who want to use you to recover from the shock of a break-up.

Alice, 27, shares her story. "My problem is big. At my age, I do not have a boyfriend. I am not dating any man. The last boy I went out with ended in disaster. He was a 28-year-old good-looking man. He had a very good job and came from a very good home. He slept with me just the first month of going out, something that I am not proud of. But something also happened. We were out together in a restaurant one evening when this girl, very beautiful, fair and about the same height as I walked in. She claimed she was his girlfriend, stormed in and began to attack both of us. Fred had not told me he had a girlfriend, but he did not seem surprised either. When I asked who this lady was, Fred said, he was not interested in her anymore. I left the restaurant in anger and with speed to save my own life. It has since left me angry. I have no interest in any man anymore. The way this relationship ended has badly damaged my already fragile confidence and spirituality. Dad, what should I do?"

Dating anyone is like tossing a coin. You can land a tail or head! Never think you will always land heads side up! That is exactly what happened to Alice. You never know where this person is coming from. You have no idea what they have been through. You have no idea what they have not revealed to you.

"Dating is indeed hard!"

WHEN THEY INSIST, 'IF YOU LOVE ME, SLEEP WITH ME'

One of the main reasons people get it so wrong about the choice of spouse, is the inability to spot the obvious and subtle red flags. I hear many good-looking young Christians put pressure on their girlfriends or boyfriends to sleep with them as proof of their love. This is not just blackmail; it is also a red flag. **Remember you are not married yet, if they insist on you sleeping with them, they are forcing you to disobey God!**

Once you sleep together, you become blind to his or her flaws. You become more interested in what is physical. Your sensitivity to glaringly obvious red flags is greatly reduced. This is when you have yourself to blame if you fail later in the marriage.

Lucy, 31, says "The reason why my first relationship did not last was that I refused to compromise with my boyfriend. He kept saying we should 'test-drive'. When I had concerns about him, he would not answer and gloss over the questions. It turned out that he was secretly dating another lady in the church. He also had a child with another lady he dated and did not marry her. I thank God I saw the signs and left without compromising."

Few things you should bear in mind...

Dating is NOT marriage; it is therefore not the time to:

1. Engage in sexual gratification
2. Be sharing a bed
3. Buy expensive items together such as a house
4. Go on vacation together
5. Cook and wash for the man

In Christianity, dating is considered just the first step singles take to study and observe each other. A determining phase where their values, beliefs and expectations are checked for compatibility with each other, enabling them to marry in future. It is therefore not considered as a marriage. The church, therefore, does not only disagree with any sexual activity during dating, but it also disciplines members found to be doing that.

> ***"Once you sleep together, you become blind to his or her flaws."***

WHEN THEY LIE TO COVER UP

The grace of discerning is required when dating a man or woman. People can lie through their teeth. Not only that, but you must not think that the person you are dating is perfect. As you also have your imperfections, so do they. It is normal. But you must know what you can bear and what you cannot bear.

Jane told her story, "When I met James, I said to my parents, I have finally met my angel and love! We went out a few times. Then I discovered this. James had no legal stay in the country. In addition, anytime we went out, he either forgot his wallet or he was expecting his next paycheck. I was paying for everything. When I questioned him, he said all her former girlfriends paid up when they went out. For me, that was a red flag. Straight away, I quit the relationship."

Dating is not marriage. You can end it anytime if you have not exchanged anything valuable, and that valuable thing can be sex, expensive gifts, trading your values and more.

WHEN YOU ARE DATING WITH FEAR

Your relationship should give you joy and excitement most of the time. If you are dating with constant fear, chances are you are in the wrong relationship. What does the Bible say?

> *"Such love has no fear, because perfect love expels all fear. If we are afraid, it is for fear of punishment, and this shows that we have not fully experienced his perfect love."*
>
> 1 JOHN 4:18 NLT

Even if you argue over an issue, it should not make you afraid of the person or your position. It is healthy to be able to express yourself in every matter while dating. Be your very self.

If you always suspect you are in a bad relationship, you are probably in one.

Signs include:

- You are not comfortable with their behaviour or attitude
- There is something you cannot put a finger on about this person
- You are deeply concerned but you cannot say
- You fear he or she is not the best deal for you
- You are not sure this relationship will end in marriage

These are all red flags. Don't wait until someone tells you or something terrible happens before you quit. Your relationship should give you the peace of mind. This should guide your heart and mind!

> ***"Even if you argue over an issue, it should not make you afraid of the person or your position."***

WHEN DATING WASTES YOUR TIME AND OPPORTUNITIES

One important commodity that young people waste in life is Time!

Many young people stop whatever they are doing to date a girl or a boy. They will be on the phone, face timing, or out every night. They forget their books. They forget their family. They forget their career. When it does not work, they put themselves in trouble. One of the most difficult things is failing your exams or getting sacked from university because you did not pay attention to your studies or books.

Nathan, 21, says "When I met this girl at Uni, I was enchanted by her beauty and charm. When she agreed to go out with me, it was the best day ever. I decided to do whatever it takes to keep her. Not only did I stop learning, but I also spent all my money on her. I had to take up a Monday to Friday job to cater for her. I blame myself that I was kicked out of school. I attempted my exams twice and failed both times. She completed university with a nice degree. I have none. She doesn't even talk to me anymore. I feel so stupid for letting down my guard as a boy from a Christian home."

WHEN DATING BECOMES VERY STRESSFUL

In the early days of your relationship, you find each other attractive and irresistible. But as the dopamine levels, the reward hormone which comes from being around them wanes, you begin to see their flaws and weaknesses

At this point, love moves from being "blind" to being "careful". You begin to see a lot of flaws which then create dissatisfaction and discontentment. This can lead to disagreement and argument in the relationship. Insecurities begin to creep in, and you begin to doubt if he or she is the right person to marry.

Mary, 22, says, "Josh and I have been dating for 18 months. We have broken up twice. There are days I want him badly. But there are weeks I am considering if this is worth the effort. It has been an emotional rollercoaster. Some days my head spins, my palms are sweaty, and my heart races just at the sight of him. I don't know if that is what everyone experiences or just me. I never knew dating someone is that hard. I am trusting God to give me peace in this relationship."

It is not just Mary. Relationships are hard. It will be even harder when you marry them and share the same space. Your relationship with him or her mimics what is ahead in the future. But you should not be too afraid. Both of you will mature together and hopefully appreciate each other's strengths, instead of looking at their weaknesses. But if their flaws and behaviours give you nightmares whilst you do not live together, the chance is that you will not cope well if you marry them. This one may also be a red flag!

> ***"One important commodity that young people waste in life is TIME."***

DATING SECRETLY

You are dealing with someone you don't know too well. Some people are in it just to take advantage of you. Either to sleep with you or take what you have. Your pride. Your dignity. Your purity. Your innocence. It could be your money. Your visa. Your property. You never know.

Be careful you are not blinded by love into making risky decisions to travel to meet persons you met online, face timing or social media. The stories of people losing their money, dignity and life, are too much to bear.

Christine, 29, says, "I travelled to Africa to marry this guy I met on Facebook. He sounded so genuine and humble. I took a loan to marry him. I took another loan to bring him over to the UK. I only realised he was gay when he came over. He would not sleep with me and gave excuses after excuses. In the end, I saw him going to a club when I was working the night shift. It cost me £15K to get him to the UK. I am demanding he pays me, else I will give him over to the police or immigration."

Internet and online dating are full of unbelievable stories. Men who conned women ostensibly to marry them even though they are already married. Not all images and photos you see online are the real people. Catfishing is the terminology!

When you are making any decisions that can be costly, it is wise to run them by your parents, mentors or more mature people. Relationship breakdowns are common and have led to many heartbreaks.

DATING CAN BE UGLY

When you meet a person who has been bitten by a relationship snake before, it is easy to spot how they approach their next relationship. It reminds me of this African proverb, "once bitten, twice shy". They refuse to try any drink that has the same colour as their last poison!

Such people refuse to put all their eggs in one basket. Too many people enter relationships with all that they have. In fact, they completely give themselves away to their boyfriend or girlfriend even before they say I do.

They go on holiday together. Some go on ***'bae-cations'!*** Others completely submerge themselves into this relationship as if they are already at their destination. You will see them walking together at every programme at night and in the day. They ignore warning signs. They ignore advice from family and friends until one day, it all comes crashing down.

That's exactly what happened to Matthew, 34, and single.

"I thought I was the luckiest man on earth when I found this lady. We went out for three years. We were planning to buy our house before we married. I had no reservations about her. Then I found out by chance that she had no womb. She also had a chronic genetic condition. By this time, we were sleeping together and had also made several promises and covenants never to leave each other. My heart was torn into pieces. I was so disappointed it got me into depression. I wouldn't eat, sleep nor go out. I didn't also want to talk to anyone. It took the intervention of my friend Bob who stood by me in prayers. By the grace of God, after 6 months of depression I am almost back to my best. But it has left me traumatised. I don't know if I can trust anyone else."

You must protect your heart. You need to be careful because there are so many surprises in life. When you are dating, remember you are not yet married! Guard your heart because once it is dropped and shattered by the so-called lover, it is almost impossible to get all the pieces together to their original state.

It is not to say that all people are after you to take advantage of you. There are great and amazing people out there, who will genuinely love you. Just be discerning and prayerful in your choice.

SIX THINGS TO DO WHEN YOUR RELATIONSHIP FAILS

I have witnessed firsthand the effect of broken relationships on people. This is not always easy to bear but rest assured that if yours has not worked, you are not the first, nor the last. It is estimated that 72% of all first-time relationships fail within a year. Should I kick myself hard? Probably not. The following are some of the things you can do.

1. Accept it is not meant to be

Accepting that both of you may be better for someone else will ease some of your pain. You are not created to marry a specific person in life. If this relationship fails it does not mean you have failed in life. Look on the brighter side, you are still yet to meet a person who is made for you.

2. Give thanks

What does the Bible say?

> *"In everything give thanks: for this is the will of God in Christ Jesus concerning you."*
>
> 1 THESSALONIANS 5:18 KJV

It is said that hindsight is a wonderful thing. If we were privy to what is ahead, we would calm down and be thankful. Sadly, we do not have such privileges. When you pass your exams, give thanks. When you fail your exams, give thanks. When your relationship works, give thanks. If your relationship does not work, give thanks. You never know what God is saving you from.

3. Don't be too critical of yourself

It is natural to try to dissect and digest why your relationship did not work out. Sometimes there are obvious reasons. But many times, too, there might not be. If you find the reason, learn from it and press on. If you do not find anything, do yourself no harm. Even if you feel you lack something, don't worry too much. When people love you, they like your strengths and flaws. If they cannot tolerate your flaws, the chance is that they do not love you.

Grace says "When my 2 – year relationship with Ollie ended abruptly, I grieved! I was crying all day, all night. What was worse, I began to doubt myself, if I was good enough for anyone. I would stand in the dressing mirror and check what was wrong with me. This affected my confidence and self-esteem so badly that it took another three years before I could enter another relationship. My friends and prayer are the two key things that kept me alive."

4. Ask God for grace to let go

Relationship breakdowns at any level feel like a big loss. It feels like losing a dear one. It hurts. It is bitter. It is difficult to bear. But the Lord makes grace available to you. First to forgive yourself. Secondly, to forgive your friend. Thirdly, to let go! You cannot hang onto someone who doesn't want to be with you. He or she is not for you. Let them go!

5. Avoid rushing into another relationship

You are feeling lonely. You are feeling miserable. You also want to prove a point to them showing you are still desired by other people. There is a higher chance of falling into another relationship when you are so vulnerable. Seeking a replacement here and there can be the worst decision.

Philip, 23, said, "When Sally left me, I felt so bad and miserable. Two things were going through my head. First, I hurt myself.

Secondly, I hurt her as well. Within four weeks, I found a new girlfriend in the church. A person Sally knew very well. I clung to her. I would intentionally walk past Sally with my new girlfriend. I was so demanding that this girlfriend also left me. She realised my insecurities and that I found comfort in her. She told me to heal from my past first. That left me more traumatised. She never came to me again. The lesson I learnt was that I should have taken my time to heal. There should be no revenge whatsoever."

Recover from your wounds. Seek no vengeance. Do not do anything silly. Whatever you do now will affect you tomorrow. There are still many fish in the sea. Don't rush to go fishing when you are not seeing well.

6. Seek help

It hurts. It feels quite bad and humiliating. You are praying. You are doing everything you can, but you are still struggling. It is time to confide in someone who will listen.

Do you have family members or close friends around? You may be surprised at how they will feel for you and support you. They have been here before. They understand how you feel. They will not judge, nor condemn you. Just open up to them. All these people have been well placed to be your support and anchor. Do not suffer in silence. It is no shame for your relationship to fail. So open up. Speak up!

CHECKPOINT

Your first or second relationship did not work. List three things you did that helped you.

"You cannot hang onto someone who doesn't want to be with you. He, or she, is not for you. Let them go!

www.ingramcontent.com/pod-product-compliance
Lightning Source LLC
Chambersburg PA
CBHW021222090426
42740CB00006B/330
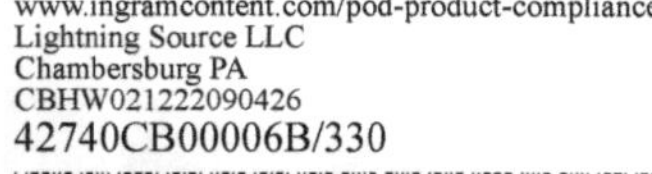
* 9 7 8 1 9 1 6 6 9 2 3 6 7 *